"Jamie's honesty and willingness to share all of the beautiful and brutal parts of foster care are so refreshing and encouraging to me as a fellow foster mom. If you are brand-new to fostering or have been fostering for a decade, this book will resonate deeply with you, give you loads of practical advice for the many difficult situations you'll encounter in foster care, help you feel like you aren't alone, and point you to Jesus on the really hard and exhausting days."

Crystal Paine, foster mom, blogger, podcaster, and *New York Times* bestselling author

"When it comes to encouraging and equipping parents on the foster care journey, Jamie Finn deserves your full attention. I laughed, I cried, I was inspired, and so much more as I read *Foster the Family*. This is the personal, heartfelt, and inspiring book we need to move us into action. Whether you're new to the foster care journey or a seasoned veteran, this book needs to be on your shelf. You will read it again and again."

Mike Berry, author of *Winning the Heart of Your Child* and CEO of The Honestly Adoption Company

"Foster parents, adoptive parents, parents of any kind, *Foster the Family* is a book you will want to read! With real-life stories and practical gospel teaching, Jamie Finn shares openly about the joys and challenges of living out the abundant life here on earth. She reminds us of our ultimate purpose as foster parents and, hint: it's not about the kids! Read this book and let it change your perspective and drive you closer to the heart of God."

Jami Kaeb, founder and executive director of The Forgotten Initiative

"*Foster the Family* is a beautifully written story, straight from the heart of my good friend Jamie Finn. Jamie is a masterful storyteller. Her thoughtfulness, vulnerability, and honesty will bring insight and hope to all who read this work of art."

Kristin Berry, author of *Keep the Doors Open*
and co-creator of The Honestly Adoption Company

"This is the book all Christian foster parents need. Jamie Finn writes with wisdom born of experience and the authority of a woman deeply rooted in her faith. You will be encouraged and emboldened in your foster care journey."

Lisa Qualls, coauthor of *The Connected Parent*

"Jamie masterfully pulls back the curtain of her foster parenting journey for us all to see what the beautifully broken journey looks like—in real life and in real time. Through raw and real stories filled with deep hurts and profound hopes told in a resonating voice that helps put words to your experiences and emotions, you will see yourself throughout. Your heart will be encouraged, your soul will be filled, your mind will be renewed, and your resolve to press on will be strengthened."

Jason Johnson, author of *Reframing Foster Care*

"*Foster the Family* is truly a gift to the world of adoption and foster care. I highly recommend this book to every person in the adoption triad. As an adopted person, I was tremendously blessed by this book. Author Jamie Finn offers a welcoming hand to struggling and prospective foster parents. Jamie's biblical teachings are like markers along the way, reminding readers that prayer and God's Word will deepen peace and that total surrender to Jesus is the answer to every human struggle."

Sherrie Eldridge, author of *Twenty Things Adopted Kids
Wish Their Adoptive Parents Knew*
and host of *20 Things Adoption Podcast*

"*Foster the Family* is packed full of honest reflections, actionable wisdom, and heartfelt encouragement for anyone who is in the foster care journey. Jamie has such a huge heart for everyone involved in foster care—foster parents, kiddos, birth families—and you can feel her warmth and love come through the pages as you read. This book is a must-read for anyone currently involved in foster care or for those considering it. You need this book!"

Jenn Hook, coauthor of *Replanted* and executive director of Replanted Ministry

"Just wow! This book is truly something special. Are you a foster parent who needs to feel seen and supported? This book is going to be a priceless gift to you! Are you considering becoming a foster parent? I believe this book will inspire you and prepare you to take the next step if this is where God is leading you. Are you simply curious about what it looks like to be a foster parent? Jamie's stories will grip you and move you and maybe even tempt you to 'taste and see' why foster parenting is worth it. The Finns' foster care journey is told with raw and powerful storytelling, and it is deeply rooted in the truth of Scripture. I wholeheartedly recommend it."

Jeannie Cunnion, author of *Don't Miss Out* and *Mom Set Free*

"Be prepared for your perspective of foster care and God to shift. While reading this book, you will be challenged and met in your challenges. You will be uncomfortable and comforted."

Tori Hope Petersen, former foster youth and the nation's leading foster care advocate

foster
the
family

foster the family

Encouragement, Hope,
and **Practical Help**
for the **Christian Foster Parent**

JAMIE C. FINN

BakerBooks
a division of Baker Publishing Group
Grand Rapids, Michigan

Published by Baker Books
a division of Baker Publishing Group
PO Box 6287, Grand Rapids, MI 49516-6287
www.bakerbooks.com

Printed in the United States of America

Library of Congress Cataloging-in-Publication Data
Names: Finn, Jamie C., 1984– author.
Title: Foster the family : encouragement, hope, and practical help for the Christian foster parent / Jamie C. Finn.
Description: Grand Rapids, MI : Baker Books, a division of Baker Publishing Group, [2022] | Includes bibliographical references.
Identifiers: LCCN 2021035427 | ISBN 9781540901866 (paperback) | ISBN 9781540902009 (casebound) | ISBN 9781493434428 (ebook)
Subjects: LCSH: Parenting—Religious aspects—Christianity. | Foster parents—Religious life. | Child rearing—Religious aspects—Christianity.
Classification: LCC BV4529.16 .F56 2022 | DDC 248.8/45—dc23
LC record available at https://lccn.loc.gov/2021035427

Published in association with Illuminate Literary Agency, www.illuminateliterary.com.

Baker Publishing Group publications use paper produced from sustainable forestry practices and post-consumer waste whenever possible.

22 23 24 25 26 27 28   7 6 5 4 3 2 1

For my husband, who's sacrificed so much for this book
and this ministry and this foster care life.
Your partnership makes it all possible;
your love keeps me going.

* * *

For my parents, who taught me that I can do anything but
that the only things worth doing are done for Him.

Contents

Acknowledgments

To Alan: Choosing to spend my life with my fourteen-year-old crush turned out to be a great decision. I'm so glad you are my partner in all of this, and I'm so grateful for the partner that you are. Your love is sacrificial and selfless, and our family unit depends on you to fill in my gaps and pick up my slack in all the ways you do. I am convinced you are the most supportive and devoted husband ever to have lived. I'm not who I am—and none of this exists—without you. I love you.

To Liv, Wes, Bella, Em, and Jax: Each day, I get to wake up and be Mom to the greatest kids on earth. Being your mom is my greatest privilege and the happiest, sweetest part of my life. Together you've taught me so much about God and motherhood and love, and those lessons pepper the pages of this book. You've sacrificed so much for this mission of other children and their families, and I'm so grateful for that. I love you forever.

To my parents: All that I've learned about childhood trauma and broken families has made me all the more grateful for the extremely loving and blessed life you gave me. Your love is unconditional and supportive, and you set the foundation for all that I know about life and love and God and family. From editing my college papers to babysitting the kids while I wrote, from teaching me the Bible to instilling in me confidence and purpose, this book doesn't happen without the both of you.

To my brothers and sisters: Josh, Justice, Jayme, and Hannah, walking this road with you is such a privilege. The way you challenge and encourage me shapes who I am, and the way you support and come alongside me shapes what I do. You're my best friends and favorite people. To my nieces and nephews: Thanks for being my kids' best friends and partners in crime. You guys are the best.

To my Finn family: Mum, Dad, Anna, Becky, Betsy, Chris, Bella, and Finn, I love you all, and I'm so grateful for you. Thanks for your support of this book and my work. And thanks especially for the parts you each played in making my husband the man he is.

To my friends: Amy, there's maybe no one else who's been as supportive of this book as you. Thanks for always being my partner in shared burden and mission and now in writing. Julie, thanks for walking as my faithful friend for so long. Your friendship has made me more like Jesus, and you've challenged me to be a better wife, mom, and friend. You both love me so well and are two of my biggest cheerleaders. To so many other friends: My early-momhood playgroup girls, my Resolved girls, my SGC and (many different) community group friends, my Admin mamas, my CARE and FosterLove friends, you have shaped my convictions and my heart and my life in so many ways.

To my partners in ministry: Jesse, Jenna, Juls, and Roxy, thank you for coming alongside me in this mission. Thanks for your love for foster families and children and thanks for your love for me.

To my pastors: Warren Boettcher and Tim Wolf, outside of my family, you've taught me more about knowing and following God than anyone else. And to Sovereign Grace Church—you are my family, thank you for twenty-three years of love and fellowship.

To the people who made this book possible: Tawny Johnson, thank you for believing in me and this book enough to fight for it. Baker team, thank you for your enthusiasm for this book and your commitment to excellence in helping me bring it into the world.

To the *Foster the Family* readers: Thank you for following along, reading, supporting, and encouraging for the past six years. This book is for you, and I pray that it serves you.

To the twenty-five-plus children I've had the privilege of mothering through foster care: I love you and remember you always. And to their parents and families: I'm grateful for the lessons you've taught me and the relationships we've shared. To my darling girl, JoJo: I miss you every single day.

To my God: All of this, oh Lord, is from You and through You and to You. To You be the glory.

Welcome to My Life

My eyes bolt open. Still hovering between asleep and awake, I fight to remember what I'd been dreaming about. Whatever it was, I think my kids were screaming. As I retrace the memory, I hear it again and realize it's the actual sound of my actual kids downstairs screaming. Squinting, I dial in to the muffled sounds from below. *Are those happy screams? Are they playing?* "That's mine! I hate you!" I hear. *Nope.* I hop out of bed, hoping the toddler asleep in the crib across my room isn't disturbed by my urgent steps—or by the screaming downstairs.

The sleeping toddler was a baby girl of five months when New Jersey's DCPP[1] called about placing her. But that was about eighteen months ago, on Christmas Day. My husband and five kids, which included our foster son—a two-year-old boy with the biggest, brownest eyes you've ever seen—were opening presents by the tree. Not only was it Christmas, but the next day was my husband's birthday. I thought it might be a hard sell, so I put on my best doe eyes. "Babe, it's Christmas. She's at the police station. She needs a home."

It didn't take much convincing. "Yeah, of course. Tell them yes," he replied.

When they brought her over, she lay asleep in her car seat for an hour while we all circled around her, commenting on her long fingers and pink eyelids. Rule number one of foster parenting (and, of course, parenting): Never wake a sleeping baby. She used to sleep through anything, but not anymore. Now I had to tiptoe.

Two of the other four kids (who shall remain nameless to protect the guilty) are awake and fighting over an old prepaid phone that lost its minutes and ability to charge (not to mention *worth*) three years ago. I rub my half-open eyes and start in with my best "gotcha" parenting. "Girls, what do you love more—the old phone that doesn't work or your sister?"

One characteristically looks at the ground and shuts down, silent. The other characteristically stomps off to her room and screams, "The phone, stupid! I hate this family! I wish I had another family!" Right on cue, the toddler starts to cry upstairs.

I comfort both the shut-downer and the screamer with long and silent hugs and correct them with the reminder that toys that provoke wars between siblings are confiscated for the day. It's Band-Aid parenting, for sure, but I have to get on with the morning. We have the crisis mental-health case manager coming at 9:00 and the toddler's new worker coming at 9:30. I need to get five kids bathed, dressed, fed, and hopefully no longer fighting in two hours' time. It's looking like a two-out-of-three day for me, so I choose bathed and dressed and skip my breakfast in favor of brushed teeth. Three cups of coffee and a psalm is my busy morning go-to.

The hot shower washes away the night's aches. God's mercies are new every morning, and a good shower certainly helps. These seven minutes will almost certainly be my only alone and quiet time this morning, so I think through the day, starting with the kids' assignments. We're in our first year of hybrid homeschooling: three days of classes at "school" with teachers and other kids, two days at home with me and their siblings. I used to homeschool full-time until work started to pick up, and being both a homeschooling mom and a work-at-home mom (two mutually exclusive roles) became impossible.

Work for me isn't easily defined. I write about foster care on the internet, I host a podcast, I speak at conferences. I also own a business that sells products that center around and benefit foster care. And I'm the founder and executive director of a nonprofit organization that serves local foster families. It's a little bit of a lot of different things, but it all centers around this one thing: foster care.

When I became a foster parent seven years ago, I never could have known how it would take over every part of my life. I write and talk about; fundraise, plan, encourage, and strategize for; and *live* foster care all day every day. My husband, Alan, and I talked about adoption in a "probably, one day" sort of way ever since I met and fell in love with him at the ripe old age of fourteen, but ten years in, we hadn't taken any steps. When my brother and sister-in-law adopted through foster care, we thought they were crazy, but God used them and others, along with books and Scripture, to convict and convince us. We signed on with a nervous (on Alan's part) and excited (on my part) willingness to accept one healthy child at a time on a very day-by-day sort of basis. We were going to try this thing out, see how it went. Twenty-four kids of various ages, two adoptions, and an array of medical needs, behavioral issues, and circumstances later, I'd say we're pretty much in it for life.

We approached our "yes" to foster care with our two biological kids, Liv and Wes—five and two at the time—in tow.

Since then our family has (permanently) grown by two more through the adoption of two of our foster daughters, Bella and Em. Our house has three open beds that are almost always taken up by one or two other kids as the need arises. If you're counting, that's four to six kids—four forever children and one or two temporary foster children. Right now the lineup of our five kids includes Liv (twelve, biological), Wes (nine, biological), Bella (seven, adopted from foster care), Em (six, adopted from foster care), and Jovie (two, foster). I typically subscribe to a "labels don't matter; they're just our kids" mindset, but for our purposes on these pages, I think the distinction is helpful.

As I jump out of the shower and throw on my at-home uniform of yoga pants and a tee, I get a text from the toddler's lawyer. "Are you available for a video conference today at 2:00?" I set a timer on my phone for 1:45 before even responding with "Yes." I completely forgot about the video conference that was scheduled for last Friday, and I can't let that happen again. Once may be forgivable, but twice is not. One thing is for sure: All the appointments and paperwork of foster care have confronted my forgetful, disorganized self head-on.

I get everyone dressed and fed semisuccessfully. Yes, one kid's sensory processing issues meant we had a fifteen-minute meltdown because the only pair of acceptable pants (despite the eight pairs of perfectly fine pants sitting in the dresser) was sopping wet in the washer. And, yes, one of the kids hid in the kitchen cabinet, nowhere to be found, when they heard that a social worker would be visiting. And, yes, the toddler threw an entire tray of food onto the ground while repeating—in mockery of me, I'm convinced, as I'm on my hands and knees cleaning it up—"Uh oh, uh oh, uh oh." But they're all dressed and fed.

As I get the big kids started on their schoolwork, there's a knock on the door. The crisis mental-health worker—a twentysomething guy wearing a *Star Wars* T-shirt—pulls one kid into the dining room. They talk behaviors and stressors and goals until the conversation eventually devolves into playing Nintendo together. Another knock on the door. New worker. We shake hands as she looks into the dining room and starts to introduce herself to the therapist. *Oh no, she thinks that's my husband.* "This is one of my other kids and their therapist," I explain. "You can come into the living room." Over time, the cast of workers, lawyers, and therapists so regularly in my home has become the norm.

The worker and I talk about the upcoming court hearing. She's brand-new to the case, so I actually know far more than she does. I narrate the timeline and characters and plot up to this point in an effort to get her caught up. She talks about the biological mom in a tired kind of way, like she has already given up on her.

"She really loves her," I offer, but I can only imagine how easy it is to open a case file like hers and write her off immediately.

The worker adjusts her tone to meet mine. "I hope she can do what it takes," she replies. "I'll be back next month," she adds as the therapist walks into the room to say his goodbyes too.

They look at each other again, both trying to figure out the other. I walk them both to the door. In case you've never done it, walking two completely unrelated people to the door at the same time is more awkward than you'd think. They both head out, and the kids and I jump into the rest of our day.

I practice the letter *R* with one. "What's this?" I ask, showing an image of a rug. "Rrr, rrr, rrr."

"Carpet!" she yells out, proudly.

"Close!" I congratulate.

I gather the crew for history and read aloud about the French Revolution. The kids are fascinated with the idea of a guillotine and take turns falling over, decapitated and dead. I see the opportunity for a *Les Misérables* solo. "Do you hear the people sing?" I belt as I jump onto the couch, fist in the air. "Nooo." The kids laugh. This may not be the first time I've done this.

We wrap up school and move on to nap time and screen time, bike rides and board games, snacks, snacks again, more snacks, and asked-for-again-and-denied snacks. When the timer rings at 1:45, I pick up my phone with confusion. I stare at the buzzing screen for too long, trying to remember what the reminder is supposed to be reminding me of. When I finally do, I thank myself for setting it.

I log on to the computer and prepare for the video conference with the lawyer. "Hi, Jamie," I hear through the pixelated screen. I can hear it in her voice: bad news, or at least news she doesn't want to break. She passes right over the niceties. "So, the court ordered for you to go to the prison with the child to meet Dad."

My voice sounds chipper. "Okay, that's fine," I say as I drag my palm against my forehead, forgetting for a moment that the video betrays me.

"Are you willing to do that?" she inquires, noticing that my actual language and my body language don't match up.

"Yes, of course!" I answer and look into the camera. This time I remember to smile.

When I close the laptop, the babysitter (my mom—the babysitter is my mom) knocks. I give her the rundown of the day and a few guidelines: "They already had screen time, so outside time, please. And Alan will be home by 5:30 with dinner, so don't worry about feeding them."

"Sounds good," she agrees as the kids circle like seagulls.

"Mom-mom, look! Mom-mom, come here! Mom-mom, want to see?"

"One snack each," I say firmly as I walk out the door. She already knows the one-snack rule, but I say it for the benefit of the listening kids, who are sure to pester her for two or three or ten.

Today's work is my day job, so to speak, working at the Foster the Family offices. My team and I serve a network of two hundred local foster families through emergency and holistic care. The emergency care occurs immediately after a foster family welcomes a new child. One of our on-call volunteers visits our office and builds a FosterCare Package of new clothing, supplies, hygiene items, and special comfort items for the specific age, gender, and needs of the child who was placed in the foster home. They also deliver a homemade meal and information about our resources. That's where the holistic care comes in. We host support group meetings, respite babysitting nights, trainings, and special events. We have a helpline and offer mentorship, we throw parties and buy gifts, and we send care packages and deliver supplies. Really, what we do is provide a context for foster parents to find community and receive support. Serving alongside our staff of six and volunteer force of fifty takes up much of my time, brain capacity, and heart.

As I drive to the office, I get a notification on my phone that one of our families is out of diapers, wipes, and formula and can't get to the store because the whole family is sick. "I've got this one," I text my director of operations. I'm usually stuck behind a desk or sitting in meetings, so I don't often get to serve foster families hands-on. But this family lives five minutes from me, and I need a periodic feet-to-the-ground reminder of why we do what we do, so I decide to tack it on to my drive home.

Afternoon turns to evening through the window above my desk. I pack up the bundle of baby necessities for the local family, making sure to grab a fun surprise for each of the sick kids.

Car rides—empty, alone car rides—have become my happy place. I listen to my favorite podcast as I head to the house of the foster family. I don't want to disturb them (or get sick), so I drop the package on the doorstep and send a text before driving home. "I left everything at your door. Feel better soon. Reach out if you need anything at all." It's official—no one else needs me for the rest of the day. I turn on my music and head home.

Alan pauses the basketball game as I walk in. I get a rundown of the kids' day. Highlights include a meltdown over mac and cheese, a blowout diaper, a fifteen-minute search for the remote that was both hidden and found by the same kid, one child's nightly panic attack about brushing teeth, and a night terror. But, of course, highlights also include sidewalk chalk with Mom-mom, a dad-versus-kids game of soccer, grilling and eating on the deck, and an '80s kids' movie with popcorn. A normal day, really. Equal parts challenging and exhausting, blessed and sweet. Alan shares about his workday, and I share about mine. He reaches for my hand and smiles, saying, "I'm proud of you," like he does at the end of most days.

As we crawl into bed, Alan notices the light of my iPhone. "What are you doing?" he whispers.

"I have to post something on Instagram real quick," I reply. It's not an unusual answer. Some people may consider social media a time waster, but it's an important part of my job. Sharing about my life and about foster care on the internet each day leads me to contemplation, readjustment, and worship. I pull up a photo to post, and my cursor blinks in expectation. I think through the day with all its busyness and challenges. I think about how abnormal some of the "normal" parts of our day are. I think about how hard it can be to have kids who are affected by mental illness, drug and alcohol exposure, trauma, and neglect. I think about how much I sometimes want "the system" out of my home and my day. I think about how exhausting and endless this work of supporting other foster families and children can be. I think about it through the lens of all that I know, all that I've come to learn, all that I believe, and I begin to type.

> My path into brokenness began with a prayer: God, break my heart for the things that break yours. He broke my heart. And he broke the lie that this life is about me and my happiness, broke the quest for a perfectly average life, broke the desire for ease and success and passing joys. There's great beauty in a life of brokenness-by-decision: A shattered heart seeping out the sacrifice of praise. A life cracked open and poured out in worship to Him. An invitation for God Himself to make me whole.
>
> #brokenandbeautiful #fostercare #fostermom #fosterthefamilyblog[2]

I turn off my phone and place it on the bedside table. I roll over and whisper, "Alan?"

"Yeah?"

"I forgot to tell you one thing. I emailed our worker today and told her that we're ready for another placement."

He makes a sound that's hard to distinguish in the dark but that I know is a laugh. At least I hope it is. I'm sure if I could see him, it would be accompanied by an eye roll and a conspiratorial smile. "Okay," he whispers.

I kiss him on the forehead and rest my head on the pillow. Time to get a good night's sleep. Tomorrow we do it again.

Introduction

I was big into Shakespeare as a teen. Now, before you get the wrong idea about what kind of teenager I was, you should know that this was right around the time Leonardo DiCaprio and Claire Danes played Romeo and Juliet. My obsession may have had less to do with the Bard and more to do with the Heartthrob. Whatever my introduction to sixteenth-century theater, I was hooked. I consumed every Shakespeare play, moved on to the sonnets, and landed in the biographies and commentaries and literary criticisms.

It was there that I learned that when Shakespeare wanted to communicate something and couldn't find the right word, he would just make one up. And he didn't make up one word. He invented-as-he-went seventeen hundred words that you and I use on a daily basis. Words like *arouse* and *rant* and *negotiate* and *lonely*. *Lonely*. Can you imagine the English language without the word *lonely*?

To my little budding writer's heart, making up a word you thought should exist was about as presumptuous and beautiful a concept as I could imagine. It still is.

I'm no Shakespeare. I officially "nose goes" the job of choosing the word. But there needs to be a word, just for foster parents, that says it all. We need a word. Something that encompasses every conflicting emotion and thought and experience without all the caveats and *but*s and *I feel A and also B, and I think I'm supposed to feel C*s that typically pepper our speech. *Bittersweet* doesn't cut it. *All the feels* has been hijacked by teenagers, who have not, in fact, felt all the feels. We need something else. A guttural, can't-be-put-into-words expression that gathers up the depths of every contradictory thought and emotion all at once.

Being a foster parent means that nothing just makes sense anymore. It means we can no longer sort thoughts and feelings into wrapped-up, pretty packages. It means spending much of our life confused and conflicted and overwhelmed. Half the time we don't know what we want. Most of the time even our prayers are perplexed. We regularly wade through the depths of opposing experiences.

It's all so much, I just want someone to tell me, "Here's how you should think. Here's how you should feel. Here's what you should do. Now, go on; you've got this." It may still be hard, but at least I would know what I was doing.

But there's no handbook for foster parenting, maybe because no two children, parents, cases, workers, judges, plans, outcomes, behaviors, diagnoses, emotions, challenges, or overall experiences are the same. Probably because none of us know what we're doing enough to write one.

But God is kind. He has given us a handbook for life: His very words in Scripture. Thank the Lord, the Bible is more than just a how-to manual, more than a list of rules and expectations. It's a map. And not one primarily for our journey through this life, but one outlining His journey to us. It's one beautiful plot, woven by God in eternity past and touching the moments of our present days.

God's Word speaks to every part of life. Even the parts where it—seemingly—doesn't. I've never found the words *foster care* in the Bible, but I have found rich truths about God and humans, family and children, sacrifice and trust, forgiveness and love. Foster care is all throughout the Bible. God speaking to us, commanding and encouraging, teaching and comforting.

I wish foster care had a manual. It doesn't, and I wouldn't dare presume to write one. I'm not an expert, and I don't have all the answers. This book is not a how-to kind of book. It's a from-the-trenches kind of book, a wrestling-with-God-in-the-desert kind of book. Most of all, this is a tasted-and-seen kind of book. I pray that my times of digging through God's Word and searching for an answer bring you some direction. I pray that my grappling with the difficulties of this life of foster parenting produces for you some level of peace. I pray that my tripping and falling on my face allows you to avoid the same pitfalls. I pray that God meets you through reading this as He has met me through writing it.

one

What Did I Do to My Life?

We were like a group of vets sharing war stories. Like old men sitting around a campfire, patches from wars both won and lost emblazoned on hats, sharing old tales with that so-strange combination of sadness, sentimentality, and pride. Each tale sadder and stronger than the last, growing in drama and volume as the night goes on. War stories. Telling of their unseen wounds, finding communion in their shared battles.

Our gathering was all of that. Except, you know, the part about the old men and the war. It actually was just me and my gal pals lounging on a tweed couch, drinking coffee, and doling out Goldfish crackers, soothing toddler tantrums and tween dramas.

But the experience was the same. We told tales of foster care battles past and some very, very present. We exposed the war wounds of trauma and loss and hellos and goodbyes. We savored the camaraderie of shared experience, sitting with those who could understand, finding comfort in the amen-like "mm-hmms" and the laughs that said, "I see you."

The girls' grandfather OD'd. Do I tell them?

Her IQ test came back at 64. Forget what this means for school next year. What does this mean for the rest of her life? She had a hallucination last night that bad men were touching her butt.

It looks like he's going home. Well, by "home," I mean the homeless shelter.

Her therapist said it will probably be a lifelong struggle.

Mom's parents just showed up after fifteen months and are filing for custody.

Just a few friends on a normal Thursday morning, sitting around and chatting, wading through the heaviest of heavy. I shot wide, tear-brimmed eyes at my fellow soldiers/warriors/just plain old foster moms and laughed. "Guys, what did we do to our lives?"

Who does this to their life? Who chooses to uproot a "normal" one-boy-one-girl happy life for hard and broken? Who signs on for tears and sleepless nights? Who opts in for poop smears and calls to the police, for family court and social worker visits? You and I. Foster parents.

Counting the Costs

The only person who chooses a life full of difficulty, chaos, and pain is the one who has weighed the other options and decided that the benefits exceed the costs. Being a foster parent entails costs—true costs. And like line items in a budget, they add up: less time with other children, fewer peaceful morning cups of coffee, increased stress, decreased health, marital stress, days and weeks missed at work, restless nights, heartbreaking good-byes, less time for passions and pursuits, fewer invitations to dinner with friends, missed promotions, rare quiet nights in, lack of sleep.

Some costs you can see and measure. Some are imperceptible in the short term and invisible to others. Yet each cost is tangible, bringing you deeper and deeper into the red, depleted and poor and on the way to bankruptcy.

But what about the benefits? The joys: a child's laughter, good grades, reunification, adoption. The victories: *She told me she loves me. She's becoming less afraid of men. He told me the truth when I asked him. Mom said thank you. He's opening up about the past. She slept through the night. She smiled. We had such a fun day as a family. Dad has been sober for three months.*

Are these joys and victories enough? Is the math as simple as "the good outweighs the bad"? If you're new to the game, you may still be running on adrenaline and happy moments. But time and kids and parents and workers and behaviors and investigations and reunifications and failed reunifications can beat the honeymoon right out of you. And the question stands: *Why am I a foster parent anyway?*

Foster parent, this is a question you have to be able to answer with clarity and confidence, with a foundational kind of answer. You need a sustaining truth that transcends situations, conditions, thoughts, and feelings. Your reason cannot be circumstantial. It must be theological.

Worth It

I shouldn't have picked up my phone! I should've just ignored it. Why did I even pick it up? I stomped through my sister's backyard, calling the kids out of the pool. We huddled in the corner of the yard as my kids' cousins looked over their shoulders in question.

"Guys"—I looked into each of their eyes with compassion—"the worker just called, and they're coming to pick up Dom in five minutes to move him to his great-aunt's house. We need to say goodbye. Quickly."

A cacophony of little voices responded. "What?" "No!" "We're not even home!" "He doesn't even have his stuff!" "This isn't fair!"

"I know. I'm sorry. I'm so sorry. Now give him a kiss."

When the worker arrived—the same worker who had brought him to our home from the NICU, the same worker who had talked about adoption every conversation for six months, the same worker who had confirmed "there's no family willing to step in"—I couldn't even look at her.

"Judge's orders." She shrugged.

"You couldn't have followed the judge's orders tomorrow? Or tonight?" I questioned.

Her tone shut down my questioning completely. "My daughter has a dance recital."

I kissed the forehead of the boy I'd called "son" for the past six months, walked to the backyard, and promised myself, "I'm done with foster care."

"I'm done," I repeated to Alan on the phone. My husband hadn't even gotten the chance for the quick forehead kiss that I had.

"Jamie . . . we're not—"

"Yes. We. Are. Or at least I am. I'm done," was my final answer. There were too many sacrifices. Too much heartbreak. Too much loss and injustice and frustration. Too many reasons to be done.

When we got home, I clicked on the TV for the kids—knowing the screen could offer them more than I could—and sent myself to my room. I paced around the rug at the foot of my bed and allowed the tears to stream and collect at my chin. *I hate this. I don't want to do this to myself or to my kids anymore. I don't want this to be my life. I don't want to feel this way anymore. I'm done.* I finally got tired of crying and pacing and pulled out my journal. It's where my battles are fought. Feeling my feelings, thinking my thoughts, and then reorienting all that to what I know, what I believe. To what is true.

> I hate foster care. None of this is as it should be. A baby shouldn't have to be taken from his mother two days after birth. A worker shouldn't leave just a few minutes to say good-bye. A family shouldn't have their hearts broken over and over. It's not supposed to be like this. This system and this whole wide world are broken, broken, broken.
>
> But it doesn't shock you, oh God, when I shake my fist at it all. When I say, "I hate this," and I say it to you, it's said like a prayer. A faith-filled acknowledgment that though this isn't how it should be, you are above it all. A desperate cry that though I feel like I can't do it anymore, you will give me the strength. A worn-out and weary statement of faith: I do all of this for you. A held-close conviction that it doesn't matter how hard, this is worth it.

What has carried me through the hardest moments of foster care and carries me still is remembering and believing and knowing deep down that foster care is worth it. The costs and trials and pain are overcome by the value, overwhelmed by the worth. Foster care is worth it. But sometimes I need to be reminded of why that's true.

Children Are Worth It

"Mothers do hard things out of love for their children. This is a loving and sacrificial choice," I said to the woman crying on the other end of the line. You could label her "prostitute" or "heroin addict," but really she was just a mom trying to figure out how to do right for her baby. Seven months pregnant and well aware that she couldn't give her daughter the life she needed, she was looking for an adoptive family to step in. Her friend knew I could help with that and shared my phone number.

"I don't know why this happened like this . . ." Her voice trailed off.

"I don't either, and I am so sorry for the pain you're walking through right now." I tried to empathize. "But I do know one thing: God created this precious life. He is the One who formed her in your womb. He already loves her and already has a good plan for her. He chose you to be her birth mother, and He's already chosen her forever family. Her little life is precious to Him."

She continued to weep as I grew silent.

All children are precious. Their human lives are created in the image of God, mirrors reflecting the glory of the heavenly Father, likeness bearers of the Almighty.

Every child is artfully and lovingly handcrafted by the Creator. Before time began, each child was loved and cherished and planned. All children were on the heart of the Savior as He bled in love. No past abuse, current struggle, or future prognosis; no gender, race, or ethnicity; no medical diagnosis, mental illness, physical handicap, behavioral issue, or educational classification; no thing, not one thing, *nothing* steals one ounce of the divine image from a child. No label or prefix or description that marks a young soul as "other" can detract from the inherent worth of a child.

Any day—or life—spent serving precious children is one well spent.

Families Are Worth It

Today the highlight of my day is my foster daughter's video call with her mom. She kisses the phone and toddles away with it, laughing and chatting her baby language into the screen. She loves her mom, and she loves getting to talk to her mom.

After ten minutes, I confiscate the phone and get on for my turn. I talk to her mom—this stranger turned friend whom I've come to love—about the job she got at Amazon the day before. She just moved back from out of state, so she's in transition. I ask her what she's been eating.

"Don't worry, I'm eating," is her response.

"Oh yeah, what?" I wait. "Text me a list of what you need, and I'll drive it over in the morning."

"Thank you, Jamie. Love you."

"I love you too, Kelly. Say, 'Love you, Mommy,'" I direct our girl before we hang up.

If you would have told me seven years ago when I first became a foster parent that this was a conversation I would someday have, I never would have believed you. I came into foster care understanding that children are worth it but struggling to believe that families—families so broken, so far from what they should be—are really worth trying to repair.

I'll delve into this in the next chapter, so I won't belabor this point here, but the family is important because it's been called so by God. The family is a theologically rich picture of the Trinity, the church, and the people of God. The family is the divine plan for a human's physical, emotional, psychological, and relational needs to be met. It's as important an earthly institution as can be, and it's smack-dab at the center of foster care. Playing a part in foster care—in families being healed and reunited—is important work because the family is important.

Living for Jesus Is Worth It

I still remember the commencement speech at my best friend's high school graduation. It was corny and cliché, but it was almost twenty years ago and I'm referencing it in my book, so I guess it did the trick. The pastor handed a dollar bill to each of the graduates and charged them, "You have one life to spend. Spend it on what matters." It put a lump in my throat and a fire in my veins: *I don't want to waste this one life. I want to spend it for Jesus.*

For me, this is the why of foster care. Really, it's not the kids or the parents. It's something—*Someone*—else completely. I'm not a foster parent because I know that children need homes or because I believe families should be reunited or because I love adoption. I'm a foster parent because I love Jesus. Because I want my life to be lived in surrender to Him—my days spent in worship of Him. Others may worship Him as missionaries or teachers or plumbers, but I've chosen—rather, *I've been chosen for*—this messy and beautiful work of children and families. And the days when the costs are the greatest are the days when my truest worship is offered. Those are the days when foster care is less about cuddling babies and more about giving myself to my God as a living sacrifice.

The Answer

My question, "What did we do to our lives?" was said in jest, but it's one I've wrestled with, ugly and dirty. This is the answer I've arrived at: It's not really my life in the first place. My life has been ransomed and purchased. I've been bought with a price, so now I belong to God. And above and before how I follow God is the fact that He made me His follower to begin with. My life is not about what I'm doing for Him; it's about what He has done for me. And it's from this place that I follow Him into what He has called me to do. It's at this place that the costs all make sense.

You see, God does the best kind of math. His math is the kind where nothing adds up but we always come out ahead. The kind where we merely regift to Him what He gave us in the first place and are rewarded for doing so. The kind where what we sacrifice for Him now waits for us in heaven later. The kind where we deserve nothing, and He gives us everything.

In the end, this is where the line items are reconciled, where the costs and rewards are balanced. Yes, kids are worth it. Families are worth it. But do you want to know why foster care is worth it? Because it's gospel work. And living for Jesus is always, always worth it.

two

Jesus Loves the Little Children
(and Their Families)

I always say I became a foster parent for the wrong reason.
No, not the money. I mean, the whopping *dollar an hour*
to lose all sense of privacy . . . and have the state invade your
home . . . and parent a child full-time, twenty-four hours a
day . . . and pay for every bite of food and activity and article
of clothing . . . and deal with behaviors and sleep struggles
and food issues . . . and have awkward interactions with parents and workers . . . and chauffeur to therapies and appointments and visits . . . and ride the roller coaster of the court
system . . . and ultimately have your heart broken *is* tempting.
It's a pretty sweet get-rich-quick gig, if you ask me. But, no,
it's not the money.

And, no, it's not the praise either. Although the side-eyes
and "Wow, you have your hands full" and inappropriate questions are quite fulfilling. I just love being noticed. Sometimes

people are so impressed, they go so far as to point and whisper. There's a lot of—how should I put it?—recognition involved. No, it's not that either.

It was for neither of these stereotypically bad reasons that I got involved in foster care. It was another wrong reason completely. I got into foster care for the kids. And *only* the kids.

I got into foster care to protect children from their horrible, criminal, addicted, selfish parents. I got into foster care believing reunification to be the unfortunate by-product of this whole system. I got into foster care forgetting that as precious to the heart of God as children may be, families are just as precious.

Most of the parents of my kids[1] wouldn't look so great on paper with their checkered histories and family trees, medical records and criminal records, questionable relationships and failed relationships, unstable finances and housing, and a myriad of struggles and challenges. Their life circumstances wouldn't create a very pretty parenting résumé.

My family? I know how messy we can be behind closed doors, but our public family profile doesn't look so bad. My husband and I have a strong marriage. We don't struggle with addiction, health issues, or mental illness. Neither of us has anything more than a speeding ticket on our record. Our children are loving and helpful siblings, and we have a big, supportive extended family. We're financially stable and live in a beautiful home. Our family spends a lot of time together having fun and making memories. Our résumé is pretty strong.

So that means we're the best long-term option for the kids in our home, right? *Right?*

Before I form my internal argument with pros and cons and tallies and logical conclusions, I have to rewind to the beginning. To the original plan.

Family Is God's Idea

In history's story, family comes in at the very beginning. God creates the universe. God creates the world and everything in it. God creates people. And then, immediately, God acknowledges that aloneness is not good. He creates woman, forms the very first family, and commands husband and wife to "be fruitful and multiply" (Genesis 1:28).

Family is God's idea. He created it. And He talks about it, consistently and clearly, throughout His Book.

He commands husbands to "love [their] wives and . . . not be harsh with them" (Colossians 3:19) and wives to "love their husbands" (Titus 2:4). He says that "children are a heritage from the LORD, the fruit of the womb a reward" (Psalm 127:3). He commands fathers "not [to] provoke [their] children to anger, but bring them up in the discipline and instruction of the Lord" (Ephesians 6:4) and mothers to "love their . . . children" (Titus 2:4).

Imagine for a moment what these verses look like played out. They look like perfection. Like a husband and wife who are devoted to each other forever, who serve each other with selflessness and kindness, who love each other with affection and in unity. Like parents who view their children as blessings and cherish them as such, who enjoy them and teach them, who treat them with kindness and true love. Lived out, these verses demonstrate God's perfect plan for the family.

God intended for families to be together forever in love and unity. God intended for parents to care for their children and for children to be cared for by their parents. God created the family unit, and it is sacred to Him.

But sin. Sin is the destroyer of what is beautiful, the breaker of things that are whole. And it wreaks havoc on the family.

For a very few glorious verses in Genesis 2, family plays out the way it was intended, with unity and perfect, sinless love. In the next chapter, it all goes awry. In Genesis 3, before the first child is ever born, sin enters the world and the curse touches every family ever to be formed from that day forward.

As foster parents, we know just how amiss the plotline has gone. We hold the quaking bodies of infants poisoned by their mother's bloodstream. We wipe the tears of frightened children, abandoned and left to fend for themselves. We salve the wounds and tend to the broken bones of bodies abused by their God-given protectors. We cuddle the necks of half-awake, half-asleep children consumed by fears of the remembered. We listen to real-life tales of unimaginable horrors and if-only-they-could-be-forgotten recollections.

Sin has marred God's good plan of family.

Mama Bear

Have you ever really considered the term *mama bear*? We emblazon it on T-shirts and label ourselves with it proudly. But have you stopped to think about what a mama bear actually does? If a mother bear senses that one of her cubs is at risk, she will attack. She will—quite literally—rip to shreds any human or animal that attempts to hurt one of her cubs. She'll do anything to defend her baby.

The hypothetical "if anyone were to hurt my child, they would have me to deal with" becomes a whole lot less hypothetical when we sign on as foster parents. The realities of the children we love as our own being abused and neglected aren't hypothetical anymore.

The protection we feel toward the children in our care is beautiful. The anger we feel toward the people who've hurt them is natural. Those feelings can be overwhelming. But we can't be overwhelmed by them. As foster parents, we have to take to task our hearts' natural yet sinful temptations toward self-righteousness, anger, and fear.

Maybe, like me, you became a foster parent for the wrong reason. Maybe, like me, you need to reorient and remember that being a foster parent is all about God's original plan.

The Big Story

"But sin" isn't the end of the story. The story always ends with "but God."

Jesus came to restore that which sin destroyed, to repair what sin has broken. He came to make all things new. He came that we "may have life and have it abundantly" (John 10:10). He came "to seek and to save the lost" (Luke 19:10), "to destroy the works of the devil" (1 John 3:8), to "deliver all those who through fear of death were subject to . . . slavery" (Hebrews 2:15). "Jesus came into the world to save sinners" (1 Timothy 1:15).

If we don't see our kids' parents—*ourselves*—in these verses, we need to pray for eyes to see. God is about—and has always been about—redemption and restoration. It's throughout all the stories of the Bible, from Adam and Eve to King David to the woman at the well to Peter. It's the heart of the big story of the Bible, the gospel of Jesus Christ. God is about redeeming and restoring sinners to Himself. And God is about redeeming and restoring that which sin has destroyed. Including the family.

As people who've been redeemed and restored ourselves, we must be about God's redemption and restoration of the family. And yet, as parents who deeply love the children in our care, we must be about their protection and well-being.

I want an easy, clear, always-applies-in-every-situation conclusion. But there isn't one. Being committed to this calling of protecting children and striving to be a part of God's redemptive work within the family feels like an impossible dichotomy. But it's not either/or. It is both/and. Being a Christian foster parent means living in the tension.

I adopted two children out of foster care. I've testified against the biological family in court. I've advocated against children returning home. I understand that children need to be protected from their parents—sometimes forever. But above that sad reality, and informing that sad reality, is my foundational conviction that God created the family and that He longs for it to be restored.

This means that this life of foster care is about more than just protecting and advocating; it's about playing a part in restoring. This means that as much as my heart may be screaming, *How could you do this? Why are you like this? Why won't you change?* I choose to come alongside the parents I'm protecting the children from. I've delivered diapers and clothing to parents who were caring for their babies for the first time after not visiting them in the hospital for four months. I've driven hours to bring supplies and comfort to a broken mother and her child living in rehab together. And more than what I've done, I've gotten to witness what God has done. I've watched these same parents regain and retain custody of their children, get apartments and jobs, stay sober after years of addiction, and grow into loving parents.

As Christians, we understand God's perfect plan of what the family is meant to be. As foster parents, we know that, too often, parents demolish that plan. But as Christian foster parents, may we believe that God created families to be together, that His heart is for them to stay together. And may we do all that we can to be a part of Him bringing them back together.

three

Do Not Be Afraid
(When Everything Is Scary)

I am a sleep training expert. Not literally, but I've done it, successfully, more than twenty times. I wrote an article on it that went viral. I'm the mom that mom friends tell their other mom friends to talk to about their child's sleep issues. So, by my calculations, I'm pretty much a sleep training expert. And then, Mikey.

Mikey was the hardest baby I'd ever cared for. Addiction and instability and trauma had marked all three months of his little life. He didn't care that I was the expert. He and his complex trifecta of scared, sick, and sad had no respect for my self-proclaimed sleep-training-expert status. He was going to take three hours of rocking, feeding, crying, shushing, patting, and praying, "Dear God, please just make this child go to sleep," each and every night to fall asleep.

I was, uncharacteristically, more than willing to participate in this nightly three-hour event. I loved this little boy deeply. His smile, his cry, the way he only ever wanted me. And my heart broke for this little boy. His confusion, his suffering, the hardness of his short life. If he needed me to rock him, I would. If the only place he could feel safe was in my arms, then he'd stay in my arms the whole night through.

I had seen him with his mom only once before. She was low-grade high—nodding off on her daily dose of methadone—and had no idea how to hold, let alone comfort, a small baby. At one point, she nearly dropped him. I grabbed his small body and swallowed the large lump in my throat. The hour spent with the two of them together seared fear in my heart for the reunification that would surely one day come. And then that day came. The order was made. He was headed home.

The night before he left, I rocked him in my arms. He was fed. He was changed. He was tired. And he was screaming. And while I kissed his curls and prayed he'd calm down, the thought flashed in my mind: *She's going to shake him. She's going to smother him. She's going to kill him. He is going to die by her hands.*

That thought was from the pit of hell and from the realest part of my brain. I told my mind to shut up. But it behaved like my semi-obedient child, who, when I demand silence, chooses to whisper.

I was afraid. Mikey went home. My disobedient brain kept a-whisperin'.

I know what it is to be afraid for a child. But I also know what it is to not stay afraid, to not live afraid, to not be controlled by the afraidness. And isn't that almost the same as being unafraid?

The Bible Is Scary

The Bible is full of the frightening. Although it has been accused of being a boring book, it is anything but. Real-life heroes, great kings, brave women and children, just plain nobodies throughout, all face-to-face with the fear-inducing. We'd like to believe following God means the absence of danger, that a loving God would never call His children into scary things. But read the Bible, and it's impossible to go on believing this.

God regularly calls His people into the scary. You know, scary like climbing a mountain to tie up and then spill the blood of your one-hundred-years-in-the-making, one and only son. Like devoting your life to building a boat in the middle of the desert and accepting that all the animals of the world will just show up. Like being married to a man who passes you off as his sister and hands you to another man. Like approaching the city walls of a vicious enemy with the battle plan of some trumpets and a brisk walk. Like fighting a nine-foot thug with a few pebbles. Like having a sleepover with some lions. Like being told by an angel—when you're an unmarried fourteen-year-old—that you will be pregnant with God's Son. Like watching the guy you thought was God incarnate be killed on a cross with criminals and buried dead in a cave. Scary.

And there, sprinkled throughout the truly terrifying, is God's command: "Fear not." God—or someone on His behalf—says it more than three hundred times in His Book. He doesn't say, "This isn't scary." He says, "Fear not."

I'd prefer if His words were, "I'll keep you from facing anything frightening." I like to think that God cares about my comfort as much as I do. That if something makes me afraid, it must not be for me; it must not be from Him. But God doesn't promise to protect us from the scary. He calls us straight into the scary. Then He tells us not to fear.

The simple two-word command "Fear not" may feel discouragingly overly simple. If it were as simple as "fearing not," then we would all just . . . not fear. But the call to "fear not" isn't a command to just do better and be stronger. It's really not even a command at all. It's a promise, a reminder, a hold-on-tight-to-it truth. I don't have to be afraid. *Because God.*

Throughout Scripture when God's people are told not to be afraid, they're told something else along with it. Some important truth, beautiful promise, big-picture reality of God's character.

"Fear not . . . I am your shield." (Genesis 15:1)

"Fear not, for I am with you and will bless you." (Genesis 26:24)

"Fear not, stand firm, and see the salvation of the LORD, which he will work for you today." (Exodus 14:13)

"You shall not fear them, for it is the LORD your God who fights for you." (Deuteronomy 3:22)

"Fear not, I am the one who helps you." (Isaiah 41:13)

"Fear not, for I have redeemed you." (Isaiah 43:1)

It's not just that I *shouldn't be* afraid. It's that I *don't have to be* afraid.

Fear is a sort of forgetting, a focusing on the what instead of the Whom. An amnesia of just how good God is and always has been and promises always to be. Like our traumatized children—who worry each and every meal if they will be fed, who wonder with each and every drop-off if we will come back—we look at God with worried accusation: "But how can I know You'll do it again?"

If fear is forgetting, then the antidote to fear is remembering. Remembering the faithfulness of God, the character of God, the promises of God.

The Faithfulness of God

I don't know your life. Chances are you have people who love you, you have a safe home, you're not hungry, you have things that make life sweet. Chances are you can see obvious touches of God's faithfulness throughout your life. If you're feeling blessed, just stop at this sentence and make a heart list. Trace with your memory the path of God's hand weaving your story artfully, lovingly, and doused in grace. Practice seeing His faithfulness right now and each day.

The problem with lists, though, is that they never apply to everybody. Maybe you are alone, maybe you are in financial ruin, maybe you aren't safe. Here's what I know about you: If you're a child of God, I know that your life is a picture of His faithfulness. I don't know your story, but I know the most important part of your story.

"He who did not spare his own Son but gave him up for us all, how will he not also with him graciously give us *all things?*" (Romans 8:32, emphasis mine). This isn't a consolation prize. This is the ultimate faith builder. When we consider our lives' needs, the thing that stands at the very top of the list—biggest, greatest, and most impossible—has already been taken care of. Our salvation was purchased on the cross by Jesus. And this is the Jesus we're looking to for all the other things. It's like sheepishly asking your dad for ten bucks when he has already given you a billion. "All things" are nothing compared to the biggest thing He has already done.

Honestly, I don't know why God allows certain things to happen or doesn't bring about others that I think He should. But I know this: He loved me enough to send me Jesus, so I can trust Him with everything else.

The Character of God

My fingers shook as I dialed my husband's number. "Hello?"

"They removed him again." I jumped right in. "They removed him, and our license is suspended because of that stupid, bogus investigation, and they're going to bring him to some strangers' house, and strangers are going to adopt him, and we're never, ever going to see him again. And I am *not okay!*" If you pictured me walking around my kitchen in circles, crying and gasping for breath between each word, you would be right. My husband's response, through his own pained realization that our beloved former foster son may be placed somewhere else, was this: "Jamie, God is good. And everything He does is good." I hung up and I repeated it like a mantra as I continued to walk around my kitchen in circles. *God, You are good, and everything You do is good. God, You are good, and everything You do is good. God, You are good . . .*

I fall into fear when I define who God is by what I see rather than defining what I see by who God is. And who is He? God is omnipresent, everywhere all the time. God is omniscient, knowing everything from every time. God is omnipotent, having all the power ever needed for anything. God is sovereign, perfectly in control of every person and place and thing. God is immutable, never changing, because He can never get any better or any worse. God is eternal, existing from forever past to forever future. God is holy, perfect and pure, separate and unlike His creation. God is wise. God is righteous. God is good. God is merciful. God is love.

These are real truths about the real God who is really involved in every part of my life. They're not platitudes or plaque quotes. They are the most determining factors of my fate, the most decisive forces in my life and in the lives of those I love. And they are the reason I can trust in Him.

So in the midst of fear, I can speak with confidence in who He is: "When I am afraid, I put my trust in you" (Psalm 56:3).

The Promises of God

Yesterday my son promised me that he would never spill cereal on the floor again. I don't mean to call him a liar, but this kid is physically incapable of doing anything without Tasmanian-deviling his way through it. I appreciated the sentiment, but I laughed at the promise. The problem with our understanding of God's promises is that we assume they're like ours. Really, we humans should never use the word *promise*. When we promise something, we're communicating our intention, not our ability to actually bring about the promise. I can promise my kids that they can each have a cookie after dinner, but what if they complain throughout the entire meal or start throwing up or I find cockroaches all over the cookies or a volcano bubbles from the earth and our home—and by extension the kitchen and the cookies within the kitchen—is destroyed? I'm not in control of my world enough to be able to promise something and ensure I keep the promise.

But this is not the case with our God. He "is not man, that he should lie, or a son of man, that he should change his mind. Has he said, and will he not do it? Or has he spoken, and will he not fulfill it?" (Numbers 23:19). Those same character traits of the almighty God listed above are the gold backing that valorizes His promises. God can promise that He'll never leave us because He is everywhere all the time.[1] He can promise that He will work all things together for our good because He is the Sovereign One, actually working everything together.[2] When God promises, He shows up. Or He would not be God.

The dear, must-be-kept promises of my loving Father have held my head above the waves of the fears that threaten to drown me. Friend, page through His Word and find His promises and write them with ink on your hands and with faith on your heart. As my friend Amy DiMarcangelo says, "The more we know God's Word, the more we know Him. And the more we know Him, the more we find Him to be everything He promises."³ Hold tight the promises of God, and you will find them holding you.

It's Just a Shadow

When I think of living afraid, I can't help but remember a little girl I cared for. For this traumatized toddler, everything was a trigger. So many things, in fact, that we could hardly determine what they all were. We finally discovered one that had been haunting her and confounding us: shadows. Shadows everywhere, emerging and moving, abstract and unexplained. She would tremble and scream and cling in fear.

I see myself in this little girl. My greatest fears are so often the shadows. The places where I can't see, where looming intangibles take on a frightening form. Where the threat of what something may end up being is enough to terrify. The what-ifs and could-bes, the questions and worries. The shadows. But Scripture holds this promise: "Yea, though I walk through the valley of the shadow of death, I will fear no evil: for thou art with me" (Psalm 23:4 KJV).

The shadow of death is scary. Evil is scary. Parenting is scary. Foster care is scary. I don't fight the fears by ignoring the shadows. I fight them by looking away from them—to God. To the One who walks with me through the shadows, the One who is Light and drives away every shadow. To the One who has been faithful and proven His trustworthiness, the One whose character is all perfection and never changing, the One whose promises are glorious and always kept. Through the shadows, He is with me. And because of Him, I can fear not.

four

I Don't Even Know How to Pray Anymore

"Crying like a baby" shouldn't be the expression. It should be something more like "crying like a hormonal teenage girl whose boyfriend just broke up with her," because I am sure I hadn't cried like this since exactly that had happened circa 1999.

It was maybe four years ago, and I can still feel it today, like hands tightening around my neck. I was going to lose my little girl, and my body was reacting appropriately. Fear, anger, confusion, helplessness—they all come out the same way: in messy, snotty, hyperventilating tears.

I don't care how pro-reunification you may be, when you're months away from adoption and you get the phone call that, in fact, you may not be adopting your beloved child, you hormonal-teenager cry.

After a good hour or so of nursing my emotions, I realized that maybe I should try praying. My prayers were—how should I put it?—schizophrenic.

Me: God, please, please, please don't take her from me. Please let her stay.

Also me: *How could you pray for that? She'd be going to be with her mom—her real mom. Isn't that what you want?*

Me: God, please let something come up, something that changes everything and lets her stay.

Also me: *What is it that you're hoping for? That Mom will use drugs, get arrested, lose her home? Because these are the only things that would change it.*

Me: Okay, God, please help her mom be able to do what she needs to do to get her back.

Also me: *You don't mean that, you hypocrite. You think you can trick God into thinking you believe that?*

This foster care life—and the emotions that accompany it—is so confusing that I sometimes don't even know how to pray anymore. The most basic of Christian practices, prayer feels like the one part that should just come naturally. But this journey is so convoluted that it robs even the would-be simplicity of prayer.

Anyone else struggle through guilty prayers that you don't feel like you should pray? For kids to stay (or leave), for parents to fail, for family not to show up? Anyone else eke out prayers that a part of you doesn't even really mean? For visits to go well, for parents to stay clean, for workers to be blessed? Anyone else so confounded by your child's needs or case that you're not even sure what to ask for? Which services, which diagnosis, which path?

Jesus Prayed

To be honest, I'm not naturally inclined to prayer. Maybe none of us are. But combine my sinful self-sufficiency and compulsive multitasking with a family life reminiscent of the old woman in the shoe, and I think I'm particularly weak. If something goes wrong, I swing into fix-it mode. If someone's sick, I go to WebMD and scout out remedies. If something's lost, I retrace steps and send out a search team. If someone's struggling, I search for perfect words and ship a gift from Amazon. Prayer is rarely my first line of defense.

If there's one benefit to being completely out of control of my family's fate, it's that it has brought me to my knees in I-can't-fix-this concession. It's driven me to my knees in soul-surrendered prayer. When something challenging comes up, I stop and access the fix-it part of my brain, realize there is *literally nothing that I can do*, and remember: I have direct access to the One who can do anything. I don't carry the illusion of control that I once did, and it has served my soul—and my prayer life—well to be reminded of this on a daily basis.

It's my out-of-control-ness that leads me to prayer, but have you ever considered how Jesus—God Himself—consistently and faithfully prayed?

Jesus was in control of all things. Every thing and person and force on this planet was created "from him and through him and to him" (Romans 11:36). He could have made the water from the well spray right into His mouth like a water fountain.[1] He could have kept the storm from even starting and rocking the boat and waking Him in the first place.[2] He could have brought down divine revelation on the bumbling disciples who never seemed to understand.[3] Yes, He periodically used His divine power to remind the humans around Him that He was, in fact, God and to give them the opportunity to believe.[4] But most of the time—at least from what we see in Scripture—He didn't exert His divine control to change His circumstances.

You know what He did do? He prayed. He escaped on a boat to get away and be with His Father. He poured out His heart and pleaded for God to hold off the pain that the cross would bring. He lifted His face to heaven and offered the divine alternative to "popcorn prayers." This means that prayer isn't just about going to God to get things. It's about going to God to get God. Jesus regularly came to His Father in submission and relationship and worship.

So, if God Himself made prayer such a priority, what does it look like for Christian foster parents to pray for their kids, their kids' parents, themselves?

Pray God's Words Back to Him

Does anyone else remember the first time you came across the verses that promise if you simply ask, you will receive?[5]

When I was a self-absorbed and seeking tween, this verse opened up for me an unlimited realm of opportunity. Fame, fortune, pet unicorns, and dates with Christian Slater—they all could be mine. But this verse must not be true because I was praying for money and movie star boyfriends, and none of it happened for me. That's when I learned that pesky qualifier "in His will."

But what are these requests that are already in His will, and how can I figure them out? "Who has known the mind of the Lord?" (Romans 11:34). Who could ever pray accurately when God says, "My thoughts are not your thoughts" (Isaiah 55:8)?

Prayer isn't a cruel guessing game in which we have to pick a prayer between 1 and 100 and hope we get it right. God is gracious to us. He has given us the revelation of His heart written out for our benefit, His very words to guide us in our prayers. We don't have to figure out which prayers may or may not be "according to His will" because His Book outlines who He is and what He is about. We can pray with confidence that we're praying according to His will when we're praying His words.

We pray the words He Himself has provided. Thousands of words, relevant to our trials and hardships, experiences and joys. We read them and hide them in our hearts, and then we pray His words right back to Him.

When I wake in the middle of the night before court, afraid for the future, I pray, "God, I thank You that You will be with me wherever I go. Help me not to be afraid or discouraged. Please, Lord, make me strong and courageous, remembering that You will never leave me nor forsake me."[6] When I'm exhausted and wearied by my kids' behaviors, I pray, "God, I thank You that You are gentle and humble in heart, that Your yoke is easy and Your burden is light. I feel so weary and burdened, I need Your gentle guidance. Please give me the rest for my soul that You promise."[7]

Do our prayers operate as a magical "on button" for God? No. Does God often use something He hates to bring about something He loves? Yes. (See the lives of almost every person in the Bible and, most notably, Jesus. Jesus's death on the cross serves as the most compelling and faith-inducing example of this.) Without diving too deeply into the theological deep end of God's sovereign, moral, and permissive will, all it takes is a quick look at our own lives to see that God hasn't answered all our prayers, even the noblest ones. We pray for healing and salvation and restoration—all things we know that God loves— yet He doesn't always answer the way we think He should. This is where praying God's will is ultimately acknowledging that His will is far above our wisdom and understanding. Maybe the most surrendered-to-God's-will prayer of all is praying for Him to fulfill *His* purpose.[8]

When our prayers are informed by God's Word, we're praying prayers that we know reflect His heart. We pray bold and confident prayers with the faith that He will answer. But we also pray humble, surrendered prayers with the trust that He will ultimately and perfectly decide. His Word teaches both faith and surrender side by side, so praying His will means praying both faith and surrender side by side.[9]

As the sovereign Lord, He answers prayers according to His will. As limited beings, we can best seek to pray according to His will when we know His Word, conform our prayers to it, and then entrust the prayers to Him.

When I Don't Know What to Pray

Countless times throughout this foster care journey I've felt so weak that I could barely shape the thoughts to eke out a coherent prayer. Even silent prayers depend on language, and sometimes words elude me completely. In times like this, I've thrown out words altogether and relied on the Spirit to communicate for me.

> In the same way, the Spirit helps us in our weakness. We do not know what we ought to pray for, but the Spirit himself intercedes for us through wordless groans. And he who searches our hearts knows the mind of the Spirit, because the Spirit intercedes for God's people in accordance with the will of God. (Romans 8:26–27 NIV)

My desperate prayers of "Oh God, oh God, oh God" are some of the most faith-filled petitions I've ever brought before the Lord. Calling out to Him, knowing He is there, placing "it"—without even needing to define what "it" is—at His feet have marked my greatest moments of surrender. There are times that I do not know what I ought to pray for, that I don't pray specifically for any one thing. I simply cry out to Him.

The words aren't nearly as important as the position of your heart. If you feel limited by confusion or anxiety or weakness and can't even shape the language of your prayers, then just offer your heart's groan as a plea. What a sacred and surrendered prayer you offer by simply bringing your burden to God without dictating what you think He should do with it.

Asking for Pet Dragons

This next idea may appear to be in seeming contradiction to the former points, but it comes right from the heart of Jesus and creates a well-rounded picture of what our prayer life can and should look like.

When directing His disciples in what it looks like to follow Him, Jesus regularly pointed to children. For instance, in Matthew 18:3, when He laid out clearly what it takes to be a part of His kingdom, He said, "Truly I tell you, unless you change and become like little children, you will never enter the kingdom of heaven" (NIV).[10]

It's pretty countercultural for us to look to kids as our example, and it would have been even more so back when Jesus spoke these words. This isn't the typical demographic we look to for a how-to on anything, yet Jesus pointed to their example repeatedly. So, what was He getting at?

To seek direction for your prayers, consider your own kids, the things they ask for, and the ways in which they ask.[11] Over just the past few days, my kids have come to me "like little children" with the following requests:

"Can I get a pet dragon?" ("Dragons aren't real.") "What about a dog?" ("No, we don't do pets in this family.") "Okay, then what about a puppy?" (. . .)

"Can I have chips?" ("No, sorry, bud.") "Why, because I just had popcorn?" ("Yep, exactly.") Five minutes later: "Can I have chips?" On repeat until I say yes.

While getting into bed: "Can we go to the water park?" ("Yeah, sometime!") "No, I mean tonight." ("You're getting in bed to go to sleep now.") "So . . . can we?"

Asking like little children means asking without pretense, with no fear of rejection. It means asking repeatedly and incessantly. It means asking big and grand, without considering if the ask is rational or even possible. Asking like a child means not thinking and just asking.

While it's a worthy pursuit to be shaping our prayers to God's will, too often it can lead to us working to sanctify our prayers before bringing them to God. As Paul Miller says in his book *A Praying Life*, "We know we don't need to clean up our act in order to become a Christian, but when it comes to praying, we forget that."[12] I need to be less concerned with the pretense of praying the *right* way (which can easily become the self-righteous way) and focus on simply coming as a child, in faith, to my Father.

The God who knows my thoughts before I think them, who even before I say a word already knows,[13] isn't shocked by my imperfect prayers. The gospel means that I never have to get my act together before approaching God. It means coming to Him with messy emotions and selfish requests and being sanctified by Him through the praying. It means that the blood of Jesus covers even my prayers.

Flashback to hysterical me four years ago. For the eighteen months prior, I had been praying for my little girl in apologetic, unsure terms. "If it's Your will for her to go home, then please let her go home. But if it's Your will for her to stay, then please let her stay." My desire to constantly acknowledge God's sovereignty and my uncertainty about what to even ask had led me to praying weak prayers. I wasn't sharing my heart. I wasn't crying out to God. I wasn't talking to my Father. My words were thought out, self-conscious, and rehearsed. I was coming to Him like an adult.

The life-shaking news I received about adoption stripped away all the pretense of the previous eighteen months. In that moment, I was curled up before my Father, begging like His child.

As I gave in to my childlike temper tantrum turned prayer session, I discovered that as I began to truly share my heart, God began to truly change my heart. Instead of regurgitating rehearsed words, my prayers became declarations of the beautiful truths of God's character. And I started to believe them. Instead of being so afraid of asking for the wrong thing that I ultimately asked for nothing, I began praying in a way that was really just telling my God what it was I actually wanted. And I started to want what He wanted even more. Instead of carefully crafting my words, my prayers became a child's begging. And I started to trust Him as my Father.

The Quest for the "Right" Prayer

I had an aha moment when one of my former foster children left my home. I realized that before he came to our family, (chances are) he had never had anyone in his life who had prayed for him. Mom had no family and no support system. Few people even knew he was alive, let alone cared enough to pray for him. But that had changed. He had our family, our extended family, our faith family. He had—now and forever—actual children of the heavenly Father bringing his name before Him in petition. It didn't feel like much, but it also felt like everything. Prayer is the very greatest of gifts we can give to our foster children. Though it feels like there's so much to do, the very best we can do is to get on our knees in prayer. And doing so actually changes things. In this mind-blowing, big-picture plan of God's sovereignty, He actually ordains our prayers to be part of what determines His plans.[14] When Moses begged God to show mercy and "the LORD relented from the disaster that he had spoken of bringing on his people" (Exodus 32:14), God seemed to change His mind after Moses asked Him to. Prayer alters the course of reality as it stands.

Accessing the almighty God on someone else's behalf is the most effectual, loving thing we can do for anyone in our lives. But I *so want* to do it the "right" way, and prayer is just another part of my life that was flipped upside down when I became a foster parent.

What I've learned, as I've imperfectly stumbled through praying for my foster children, is that the actual content of my prayers is secondary. Prayer isn't an incantation, it's not a cryptic recitation of the perfect words. Prayer is an act of surrender. Prayer is saying to God—using His own words back to Him, groaning my heart out, or unloading childlike and imperfect pleas—that I believe who He says He is. I believe He is in control. I believe He is good. I believe He is wise. I believe He can do anything and do it perfectly. Prayer says to my God—and to myself—that I believe He hears me and will answer me.

five

Out of Control

A jolting bang on the door and two individuals standing on the doorstep. It takes a second to compute, because you can tell they're DCPP workers, but you're sure that you didn't have an appointment. And that's when it hits you. They're not here about the kids. They're here about you.

This was the second of the two investigations my family has gone through. The first was initiated by a desperate biological family member, this one a bitter DCPP worker. Both were backed by ugly motives and full of utter lies. Both were the last things on earth I ever would have chosen for my children or myself.

They take each child into a separate room and grill them. Tears stream down my face as I overhear the questions: "Do you feel safe with your mommy? Does she hurt you? Does she take care of you?" I decline a urine test and show them that we do, in fact, have food in the house. The investigation comes along with an automatic probation, a scarlet *S* of suspension tagged on to my name for ninety days.

It's just the most helpless feeling. There's nothing quite like a stranger standing in your home with the threat of taking your kids from you to make you realize, *I have no control.*

You Were Never in Control in the First Place

I should have learned my lesson from the birth of my first biological daughter. I spent nine months curating the perfect birth plan—driving an hour across the bridge to the closest birth center, taking "hypnotic birth" classes, reading every natural-birth book on the market. Then a couple of days before my due date, I lost control of half my body, and my mouth drooped in stroke-like imitation. They stuck me in an MRI machine, told me I had a brain aneurysm, helicoptered me to another state, and scheduled my C-section and brain surgery. As my husband prepared to be a single father, we received the news that, *oh, actually*, they misread the MRI and I'd be just fine. I was diagnosed with "complicated migraines," but—just to be safe—C-section it was.

My initiation into motherhood was a baptism of fire. "Welcome to motherhood. You love this little human more than life itself. You want to plan and determine the best for her only and always. But, just a reminder, you have zero control over how anything in her life is going to play out."

The lesson didn't get through. Because so much of her little life *was* in my hands, I believed the lie that my hands were the ones actually in control. I'm not even a type A, control-freak kind of person. I was just a mom who believed that if I did right for my kids, everything would turn out "right." I'm pretty sure that many biological parents live under the same illusion.

Biological parents, have you ever thought through the assumptions that you operate under for your biological children and the worries your heart projects for your foster children? Chances are, when you boil it down, you operate under the belief that you're in control of one and not in control of the other. Where does your mind go when you consider your lack of control?

- **I could lose them.** Oh, friend, you are never promised one more day with any of your children. I don't mean to be morbid or to put fears in your mind that aren't already there, but fifty-five thousand children die each year in this country from illness and accidents and I-never-thought-it-would-be-my-kid incidents. Yes, as a foster parent, you will face loss. But loss is not unique to foster parenting.

- **They might not turn out okay.** We check off lists of the diagnoses and behaviors we're willing to say yes to, and we think we can predict how everything will play out. I have a group of friends—myself included—who are all wading through the deep and hard with our foster and adopted kids, but for each of us, our most challenging child is one of our biological children. You could accept only the most perfect of foster children through placement and then birth a child who has significant medical or behavioral needs. We have no control over how any of our children may struggle or how they'll turn out.

- **I won't be able to do what I believe is best for them.** I used to be a super-crunchy health nut. I was more prone to make an onion poultice than a doctor's appointment and to hit up the homeopath shop before the pharmacy. My biological kids were vegan, and I breastfed them until they were, like, five years old (two and a half, actually, but it eases the blow of breastfeeding a toddler when you start with a bigger number). As a foster parent, I no longer got to make these kinds of decisions. Formula and mandatory medical procedures and lollipops given to babies on visits became the new norm. And you know what? Many of those kids have been healthier than my biological kids with their perfectly mapped health plans. Insert your "I won't be able to decide"—be it discipline, education, schedule, influences—and then remember: I could make all the "right" decisions for my children, and it doesn't mean that the "right" outcomes will follow.

Let's take a breather from the doom and gloom. This is not a list of "New Things to Be Afraid Of." God is a good God who loves our children, writes all their days in His book, and gives His angels charge over them.[1] This is also not a "Well, bad things are inevitable, so why try?" excuse. If you think for a moment that I'm not fighting hard to protect my kids' safety and build their health and train their hearts and direct their futures and generally do what I believe is best for them by any and all means possible, you are mistaken. I'm simply acknowledging that having children always involves risk. My biological children, my foster children—I'm really not in control of any of their fates.

Here's what this list is: a reminder to humbly surrender. Give up the illusion that you are in control of the fate of any of your children. Bring all the things that you hold with tight fists of control and lay them at the feet of your Father. Even when it seems like you're in command, even when it's easy to pretend that you're the one determining all the details, you are not. "You do not know what tomorrow will bring. What is your life?" (James 4:14).

It's easy to say, "Just let go of control." But the struggle runs so deep that the battle against it is uphill and hard. Maybe you're a self-proclaimed control freak. Maybe you're just a parent who so deeply loves your child that you don't even know how to reconcile your feelings with the lack of control you experience. No matter your inclination, the temptation to pull for control exists.

It Takes Two to Tug

I'm a bit like my twelve-year-old. She's a little mama, and she bears the joy and brunt of helping and encouraging her younger siblings. Sometimes she even babysits and she's the one "in charge." But outside of her babysitting duties, I'm constantly reminding her that she is not the mom, that she is not in charge, that this is not her job. That's frustrating for her because sometimes she *is* temporarily in charge and—let's be honest—she always thinks she knows what's best. But trying to walk in authority that isn't hers just makes things difficult for everyone, including her.

We become frustrated when we veer into a role that isn't meant to be ours. In foster care, we wear so many hats: advocate, nurse, therapist, chef, teacher, chauffeur. On one hand, it feels like we hold countless roles. On the other hand, we have one very specific role: to care for the children in our homes. My job is not to call the shots or determine the endgame. I may be the best decision-maker in the arena, I may have the clearest perspective of everyone involved, I may hold the most information of anyone. But God did not ultimately ordain "decision-maker" as my position. Unless you are your foster child's caseworker, lawyer, and judge, it's not actually in your "job description" to hold the decision-making power.[2]

At times, decision-making for my foster children feels like an ugly game of tug-of-war. All the pulling brings anxiety, frustration, and anger. But tug-of-war can only happen if I keep tugging. If I succumb to the pull, then I'm spared the physical and emotional exhaustion of all the tugging on my end. Now, I'm not talking about just going with the flow. I'm never one to sit down and stay quiet, especially when it comes to the good of my kids. Advocate, work, fight, speak—and trust. The struggle is not so much about my behavior and words; it's more about the position of my heart. If I believe God is the One who ordains authority,[3] then giving up the fight for control means trusting *Him*.

Remember Who

Giving up control is not a vague and passive opening of your hands to the wind. It's an active and faith-filled decision to surrender. And the object of our surrender is a Person: the almighty God Himself. "In *him* my heart trusts" (Psalm 28:7, emphasis mine).

Emily was the little girl who taught me this. We weren't planning on accepting another placement, but when our worker called in a panic and said, "One of our foster parents just called and said, 'This kid can't stay for another moment. Come pick her up now,'" we did just that. We drove over and picked her up.

It was an emergency placement, but Emily needed a forever family. She spent only a week with us, but I'll never forget how she looked at me with wide eyes and cried, "Scary things happen at night," as her body trembled in bed.

"Not here, they don't. No one has ever been hurt in this home, not during the day, not during the night, not ever," I assured her with confidence.

69

I'll never forget when I brushed her hair, how she looked at me with sad eyes and said, "My daddy used to brush my hair . . . before he got sick." (He wasn't sick. "Sick" was a euphemism another foster parent or worker chose for prison.) I'll never forget the turmoil Alan and I struggled through as we looked at this little girl who needed a forever family and wondered whether we were meant to be that family. We had known her for only a few days, and DCPP wanted a forever commitment. But our week together was sweet and our hearts broke for her, and—despite our uncertainty—we had the faith for a yes.

"We'd like her to stay," I told the worker over the phone. "We'd like to move forward with adoption."

"We're moving her to be with her brother," was the curt answer back. "I'll come get her tomorrow."

Wow. Okay. She should be with her brother. This is the right thing, I told myself as tears spilled from my eyes.

Fast-forward to almost a year later. I answered just another normal placement call about a little girl who needed an adoptive family. Our home was full, but I called around to a few friends to see if they were able to help. "You know that's Emily, right?" a foster mom friend responded. "She's been bouncing from home to home for the past year. It didn't work with her brother, and she's been in a string of bad foster homes since." It took my breath away. *Emily? The little girl we wanted to adopt a year ago? The little girl who should've been a forever part of our forever family by now? This broken system, failing yet another child.*

I know that Emily was eventually adopted by another family, exactly the right family for her. With the benefit of hindsight, I see now how this was good and right for her and for our family alike. But at that moment, I was confronted, again, with the brokenness of this broken system. More than that, I was confronted with the questions of what I actually believe about the God who is over and above this broken system. Do I believe He is present and involved? Do I believe He knows me and my children and what is best? Do I believe He always acts in love for His beloved? *Do I believe He is trustworthy?*

The players in this system will fail. They will misstep and drop the ball. And it can feel like our children and their families—and *we*—will lose out. But would a good God allow anything other than what is ultimately going to be good? He is the One who "in all things . . . works for the good of those who love him" (Romans 8:28 NIV). He is able to fill in every gap. He is able to bring about the best.

Fighting for control doesn't actually gain us control. We may plan the course, but the Lord establishes our steps.[4] Since we're not in control anyway, and since we are deeply loved by the One who is in control, we can give up the illusion of and battle for control and surrender it to Him.

Friends in High Places

In my role as the director of a nonprofit that serves foster families, I've had a number of meetings with New Jersey's Commissioner of the Department of Children and Families. Her boss is the governor, so let's just say that she has the power to get stuff done. Every once in a while, a foster parent friend will talk about some change that needs to happen and joke, "Can you talk to the commissioner about this?"

Having access to someone in power can feel like a golden ticket. When we have an ally in a high place, we feel like there's someone who can work things out on our behalf. Friend, hear me: You have the ear of the One who can get stuff done. God your Father gives you full access to Himself and invites you to approach the throne of grace with confidence,[5] bringing along all your concerns for all the people you love. You can scramble to get all the different players to hear your voice—and there are times that you should—but the most effective way to use your words is to raise your plea to God.

Prayer is powerful to effect change in our children's lives, their families' fates, and the direction of their cases. But it's also powerful to change our own hearts. If you feel stuck in your white-knuckled grip for control, the most surefire way to begin to unfold your fist is to pray. "Dear Lord . . ." is synonymous with "I know You've got this."

Naviphobia, or the Fear of Boats

I love the beach, but I am terrified of actually being in the ocean. I'll lie in the sand and watch from the shore, but you'll never get me past my knees in the water, let alone floating around in a boat. The vastness of the ocean and the violence of the waves and the threats that loom underneath the surface leave me feeling unhinged and terrified. Foster care can feel like that. At times I feel not only like I am not in control but like things are completely out of control. At times I want to shake Jesus and, like the disciples, accuse Him: "Teacher, don't you care if we drown?" (Mark 4:38 NIV).

I love the story of Jesus asleep on the boat during the storm because I can relate to the ignorant and doubting disciples. They've watched His miracles and heard His words and seen heaven itself open wide and declare Him the Son of God. Yet they're surprised that He can turn off the wind. "Who is this? Even the wind and the waves obey him!" (Mark 4:41 NIV). We know who He is. He's the One "who has measured the waters in the hollow of his hand" (Isaiah 40:12). The waters don't just obey Him; they were created by Him. Their very molecules were formed and are sustained by Him.[6] He brought them into existence and He holds them and He sends them where they must go to accomplish His purposes. "Whatever the LORD pleases, he does, in heaven and on earth, in the seas and all deeps" (Psalm 135:6).

Jesus said to His disciples, as He says to me and to you, "Why are you so afraid? Have you still no faith?" (Mark 4:40). The essence of faith is believing in spite of your sight. I can easily see the tsunami-like trials that are threatening. I have to fight to see—with eyes of faith—the God who is in and above the storm.

As out of control as the foster care–induced tempest you face may feel, it is, in fact, very much under control. Don't you know that Jesus is with you in the storm? That He is the One who created and controls the wind and the waves to begin with? When you're in the storm, and it feels like God is asleep on the job, remember that He is the Lord of the storm.

None of My Children Are Mine

In a very real sense, all of the children in my home are mine. In another—maybe even more real—sense, none of the children in my home are mine. They were created by God, they were given to me by God, they belong to God. I've simply been entrusted with their care—some of them for a short time, some of them for a lifetime. Their lives are safer in His hands than they could ever be in mine, and I willingly relinquish them all to Him.

And that is how I'm able to hand over control of these beloved children. I don't relinquish control to a broken system or to a flawed decision-maker. I relinquish control to God. "I know whom I have believed, and am convinced that he is able to guard what I have entrusted to him" (2 Timothy 1:12 NIV).

six

Too Attached

"Oh my goodness! She's so beautiful." The characters swap, the location changes, but the dialogue is always the same. "You're such a saint." *If you only knew.* "What you're doing is so wonderful." *Here it comes.* "But I could never be a foster parent . . . because I would get too attached." I bite my tongue and flash my tilted-head-scrunched-nosed-dead-eyed half smile. I try to assume the best, smile and nod, and use the conversation as an opportunity to encourage or inspire. But internally I think, *Well, that makes two of us.*

The ABCs of Attachment

Attachment is really the whole point of foster care, after all. Kids don't just need homes and food and caretakers. They need families, families who are willing to give them their hearts, love them as their own, and get "too attached."

We misuse the word *attachment* to mean something like "bond," but it's so much more than that. Attachment isn't a sentimental feeling (as in "I love my teddy bear"); it's a foundational skill (as in "Oh, now I understand what safety means"). The attachment cycle starts at the very beginning of every person's life. The basic gist of the psychological model goes like this: baby has a need, baby cries, caretaker meets baby's need, baby develops trust.[1] It's the cycle of every healthy parent-child relationship.

Attachment is vital to human development. The loving touch, affectionate gaze, and calm voice of a parent activate the cells of their baby's brain and promote everything from emotional regulation to a sense of self to brain plasticity.[2] As I've rocked and comforted my foster babies, I've often thought, *You may not remember me, but your brain and body will remember this. And it will make all the difference.*[3] Attachment teaches a child, "The world makes sense, my needs will be met, people are trustworthy." It's the scaffold for every other relationship a child will form and the basis of every interaction a child will have with the world around them. And it takes (at least) two people to make it happen.

Foster parent, our foster children need us to go all in, hold nothing back, and give everything we can to provide them with the gift of attachment. But this can be terrifying, can't it? What's left unsaid within the talk of getting too attached to a child who may leave is the fear of a broken heart. Behind this idea of getting too attached is the underlying question, How do I love this child with my whole heart *and* be okay with the prospect of him leaving?

No Such Thing as Too Attached

It's only natural to want to protect yourself from heartbreak. Our body's neurological pain sensors were created by God to protect us from being hurt. You touch the hot stove, you get burned, and you learn not to touch the hot stove again. Our heart's nonphysiological pain sensors can fire the same way: *This is going to hurt. Protect yourself.* But we have to fight this self-protective urge. Our kids need us to.

Attachment doesn't come as easily with children who don't have the benefit of a baseline of healthy attachment.[4] When Willow, a three-year-old girl with a wide, toothy smile and the build of a six-year-old, joined our family, she walked right through the door with confidence. This was her fifth home in three years. She knew the drill. As she played with the other kids, I commented to my husband, "She seems so happy and healthy!" A minute later, she ran into the kitchen. "Look, Mommy!" she said to me, the stranger she had met ten minutes earlier. Before she ran out of the room, she gave Alan a quick hug, "Hi, Daddy!" Alan and I looked at each other with wide eyes. What appeared to me as "happy and healthy" was more likely an unhealthy, or insecure, attachment. Yeah, she was just fine in our brand-new home of complete strangers because she didn't know where she belonged or whom she belonged to. Later that night, as we joined my brother's family on the boardwalk, Willow ran up to meet my brother and threw her arms around him. "Daddddddy!" she yelled.

Building on a faulty foundation takes twice the work. If we waste our efforts checking our emotions, fighting our feelings, and otherwise guarding our hearts, we're only diverting our energy from the most important focus. Worrying about getting too attached takes away from our ability to love and serve our foster children the very best we can.

Don't Guard Your Heart

The battle for foster care survival isn't in the heart, after all. As foster parents, we worry so much about giving away our hearts, about getting "too attached," about loving and losing. But that isn't the true concern. The heart isn't where good foster parents meet the end of their rope; emotions aren't what lead them to the breaking point. The real battleground? The place where foster parents most often meet defeat? The mind.

It's in our thoughts, daydreams, worries, and wonders that we wage war. It's in our thinking that the war is won and lost. The key to surviving foster parenting isn't to "guard your heart" (foster parent, give your heart generously to every child who enters your home). The key to surviving *and thriving*—getting too attached and still coming away whole—is to guard your mind.

Put your hand on the table (seriously, do it). Now tap your pointer finger, keeping all your other fingers on the table. Now tap your pointer finger and your ring finger, repeatedly, at the same time, while keeping your other fingers on the table. Maybe your dexterity is out of this world and you're able to do this easily. Most of us will have to focus and work to get it right.

Your two fingers are two different body parts. They have different muscles and bones, and your brain accesses different synapses to control the movement of them. But we're so used to these fingers functioning in unison that it takes effort to operate them separately. The heart and the mind are like this. Our thoughts trigger our emotions and our emotions trigger our thoughts, and—left unchecked—we follow, round and round, the cycle of this emotion-driven engine. We're so used to them following each other and working together that we forget that the heart and the mind are different and that we can operate them separately.

When I was fourteen, "Guard your heart" was synonymous with "Don't fall in love with boys." I'm not sure where this faulty theology came from, and believe me, it didn't work. I fell in love with all the boys. But Proverbs 4:23 isn't about guarding ourselves against emotions. When we look at this verse in context, we see that it has very little to do with our emotional center and everything to do with our thoughts and beliefs. "Instruction," "understanding," "learning," "teaching," "wisdom" are the words that pepper Proverbs 4 (NIV), and this verse is about guarding the place where these things take root—namely, our minds. God is not directing us to build walls around our hearts, and we shouldn't use this verse as the justification for withholding affection from our foster children in an attempt to protect ourselves from getting too attached.

In fact, I've come to the conclusion that there's no such thing as getting *too* attached. I don't believe you can give too much of your heart, love too much, provide too much care. In matters of the heart, there can be sacrifice and loss and pain, but there's never too much. I've decided to stop worrying about my heart. I've chosen not to hold and hoard but to be gloriously, stupidly generous with it. I believe love and attachment are the greatest gifts I can give to my foster children, and I give them away freely.

I can't provide a checklist for what it looks like to love your children, but I don't have to. How should you love your foster children? Remove the word *foster*, and it becomes obvious. Love your foster children exactly as any child should be loved by their mother, cherished by their father. Love them hard and fierce. Hug and kiss them, smile and laugh with them, cry and grieve with them. Take them to baseball and dance, watch movies and do puzzles, kiss their skinned knees, and tuck them in at night. Hold them in your heart, and carry them in your prayers. Treat them and love them like they're your own.[5]

Sometimes doing this will be easy, and sometimes it will be hard. In the midst of saying our very hardest goodbye to our long-term foster son, we accepted the placement of a baby girl. Grief has a way of closing your heart in unexpected ways, and my heart was completely shut to her. Our soon-to-be-gone son was boisterous and fun with mocha skin and a mop of tight curls; the new baby had a bald head and translucent skin and was as playful as any other infant (that is, not at all). He smiled and ran into my arms; all she did was sleep. *I feel nothing for you*, was all I could muster up. The deep love I felt for him stood in stark contrast to the void I felt toward her. But I girded myself for motherhood and put on love. I smiled and sang songs and rocked her in my arms the way I would if I felt the love of a mother toward her. I acted in love, I walked in love, and soon my heart was filled with love. An overwhelming, breathtaking kind of love. I did the actions of love until I eventually felt the feelings of love. My advice if it's easy? Give in to all the feelings. Don't hold back your heart. And if it's hard? Fight for it. These kids deserve to be cherished and treasured.

It's All in Your Head

You have sixty thousand thoughts a day.

I know my brain. I am not that smart or creative or *thoughtful*. Sixty thousand of anything should create a little more productivity or wisdom than I have. Honestly, if I have sixty thousand thoughts a day, a strong thirty thousand have to be about food, ten thousand about coffee alone (*I need coffee*; *This coffee is amazing*; *Where did I put my coffee? I need more coffee*—on repeat, forever and ever, amen). Our minds are thinking machines. All day every day, they produce thoughts and narratives and beliefs that shape everything else.

Friends, welcome to the battleground. Of life, of faith, of foster care. I invite you into what it's looked like for me to battle.

> We take captive every thought to make it obedient to Christ.
> (2 Corinthians 10:5 NIV)

Captive is such a strong word. It makes me think of Liam
Neeson movies and assassins and police raids. It's a powerful
image. When I take my thoughts captive, I don't let them go
rogue. I bind them to a chair and tie up their wrists, and I force
them to obey Jesus. A few of my usual suspects that need to be
taken captive? Daydreams, judgments, and worries.

Daydreams

My mom, in all her KJV glory, has reminded me more times
than I can count about "casting down imaginations" (2 Corinthians 10:5). When I became a foster parent, my propensity
to daydream ran unchecked into adoption parties and middle
names and moms looking at me with tears in their eyes asking,
"Will you please be my child's forever mother?" It is, of course,
hard to have a single-minded commitment to reunification and
family preservation when you're secretly daydreaming about
adopting another mother's child.

Now, don't get me wrong. These daydreams are very natural,
and they're not even necessarily wrong. In fact, if you enter
the path toward adoption, they embody the beautiful anticipation of an expectant mother. But until then, these thoughts are
tempting. They've tempted me to discontentment and covetous-
ness and discouragement and anxiety. They may not ever fully
stop, but we can fight to stop them in their tracks. We bind
them and take them captive and make them obedient to Christ.

Judgments

I find it very, very easy to assume the worst about biological
parents, workers, and judges. Case in point: when one of my

former foster children was removed from his mom again. They were kicked out of the shelter where they had been living because she got in a fight. Again. She told me in detail what had happened and how it wasn't her fault. I paid her lip service, but I was very sure that it *was* her fault. They wouldn't have been removing him and bringing him to me again if it wasn't, right? *Yeah right. This is what you do. You cause drama; you start fights. And it got you in trouble again.* Two days later, at the court hearing, they played the surveillance footage, they pulled a witness, and they unequivocally cleared her of any blame and sent her son back to her. I had completely misjudged her. But there have been other times when I haven't been proven wrong, other times I've been proven right, in fact. In either case, it doesn't change how ugly my judgments are. I know that I have no excuse for passing judgment on someone else,[6] but left to my default way of thinking, I'll assign guilt and motives without knowing the full story. And most certainly without remembering my own faults and the mercy I've received. So we must take captive judgmental thoughts, bind them, and make them obedient to Christ.

Worries

I can become the most creative human on earth when it comes to worrying about all the things that could possibly go wrong for my children. I do my very best creative work in the worry arena. Three of my kids have sustained broken bones since we've been foster parents. Every time it happens, I immediately think, *The doctor is going to call DCF on us. They're going to open an investigation. They're going to take the kids.* I spend the day crying and pacing and jumping out of my skin every time the phone rings. I take a very normal thing like a broken bone to the nth degree and worst-case scenario.

What if the worker . . . ? What if the judge . . . ? What if Mom . . . ? What if my child . . . ? What if I . . . ? You can fill in all the thoughts, all the places your mind has gone, all the most creative stories your worry has concocted. The answer to all of them is "Do not worry about your life" (Matthew 6:25 NIV). Worries distract us from the work of today. They tempt us to waste our hearts and minds on a reality that may never come. They create a story that we don't have grace for now and persuade us to forget that we *will* have grace, even if it is to come. They invade and push and scoot God—the God who sits on the throne of heaven, whether we're remembering that or not—off the thrones of our hearts. So we must take our worries captive, bind them, and make them obedient to Christ.

Be transformed by the renewing of your mind. (Romans 12:2 NIV)

We have a frustrating dynamic in our house that you may be able to relate to. It's always been the case, yet it surprises me each time. I achieve a task, and it immediately becomes systematically "unachieved" by the little humans who live with me. I empty the sink and fill the dishwasher. An hour later, I stare at a sink full of dishes with a look of confusion, as if I must have been transported to some other sink in some alternate universe: "I . . . I . . . I just did this. I don't understand."

Renewal is not a once and done process. When something is made new, it immediately begins the process of becoming old again. Renewing your mind is a constant rebirthing of new thoughts, of making new and making new again and making new again—always. It's exhausting work, but the fruit of renewal is beautiful: transformation. We can actually transform our lives by making our thoughts new.

Renewal is a process of removing the old and replacing it with the new. It's what the Bible calls "putting off" and "putting on." "You . . . were taught . . . to *put off* your old self, which belongs to your former manner of life and is corrupt through deceitful desires, and to be renewed in the spirit of your minds, and to *put on* the new self, created after the likeness of God in true righteousness and holiness" (Ephesians 4:21–24, emphasis mine).

To get extremely practical and simple, being "renewed in the spirit of your mind" is a process of *putting off* a "bad" thought and *putting on* a "good" one. Renewal is a process of replacing. It's the practice of taking the thoughts of the old self that we've already learned and believe, and replacing them with what we know about God.[7] We put off the lie or judgment or fear and put on the truth. "I'll never be able to say goodbye" becomes "I can do all things through Christ who strengthens me."[8] "How could Mom be so selfish?" becomes "What do I have that I did not receive?"[9] "What if . . ." becomes "All the days ordained for me were written in your book before one of them came to be."[10]

I say to myself. (Lamentations 3:24 NIV)

Remember the old cartoons with tormented characters guided by whispering angels and devils? That's how I often feel. Except, well, it never feels like the two voices share equal volume or equal time at the mic. Honestly, it feels more like the voice with the pitchfork is the one that's loud and clear, the one that's actually most "me." The angelic voice is trapped in a box somewhere, far from my shoulder and even farther from my mind.

Martyn Lloyd-Jones famously asked, "Have you realized that most of your unhappiness in life is due to the fact that you are listening to yourself instead of talking to yourself?"[11]

The book of Lamentations is a pretty bleak portion of Scripture. The author is, of course, lamenting, so no surprise there, right? On top of grieving the destruction of God's place, he's grieving his own personal trials: affliction, "old flesh" and broken bones, walls and bears, and the like. But it's in this book that I've often found great hope for foster parenting because there in Lamentations 3, in the middle of remembering his "affliction and [his] wandering, the bitterness and the gall" (v. 19 NIV)—in the middle of listening to himself—he stops. And he starts talking:

> Yet this I *call to mind*
>   and therefore I have hope:
>
> Because of the LORD's great love we are not consumed,
>   for his compassions never fail.
> They are new every morning;
>   great is your faithfulness.
> *I say to myself*, "The LORD is my portion;
>   therefore I will wait for him."
>
> The LORD is good to those whose hope is in him. . . .
>
> Though he brings grief, he will show compassion,
>   so great is his unfailing love. (Lamentations 3:21–25,
>   32 NIV, emphasis mine)

The author doesn't experience some instantaneous shift in circumstances or miraculous heart change. He simply does the work of stopping his mind from passively listening and chooses instead to "call to mind" and "say to [himself]." He begins to preach God's character to his own heart, to tell himself what he knows, even if it doesn't line up with how he feels—namely, downcast. You'll see that he is even wooed into worship, when his first person point of view, "I," shifts to the second person point of view, "you," and in the middle of talking to himself, he begins to spontaneously praise the Lord.[12]

Seeing God in the brokenness of foster care can be hard. He may seem absent and unloving. A situation may appear bleak and out of control. My mind can wander through all the ways this is wrong and shouldn't be. It's easy to ride as a passenger on my proverbial train of thought. But I don't have to sit back. I can pull the brake, drive the train, redirect the track. I don't just have to listen; I can "say to myself."

Set your minds on things above. (Colossians 3:2 NIV)

Above our human view, there's an entire "heavenly realm" (Ephesians 2:6 NIV), a whole reality that is "unseen" (2 Corinthians 4:18). We see the brokenness and injustice; we experience how foster care is not as it should be. But God is accomplishing things in and through our families that we could never imagine. Things that—this side of heaven—we will probably never know. God is weaving stories and changing lives and writing plans that we cannot now see. But it doesn't mean we don't look. We "fix our eyes not on what is seen, but on what is unseen" (2 Corinthians 4:18 NIV). We look—with our minds—to God on His heavenly throne above, working all things together for the good of those who love him.[13] We may not see or understand the *what*—and maybe we shouldn't even be looking for it—but we can certainly see the *Who* and set our minds on Him.

Answering the Too-Attached Question

If I took the time to give the whole answer to the "I would get too attached" comment, my response would probably reflect this chapter—the purpose of the attachment, the idea that, actually, there's no such thing as *too* attached. Most of all, I'd talk about the difference between the heart and the mind.

Getting too attached to a child who will most likely leave means living in tension. It means freely releasing your heart—where you love and feel and connect—but holding the reins on your mind—where you plan and hope and daydream. Foster parent, how do you balance the impossible tension of loving a child like they're your own when they're not? You keep a strong hold on your thoughts, a close leash on your worries. You keep your mind sealed up tight. But you don't ever close your heart. You keep that wide open.

seven

My Foster Child's Family
Is My Enemy

Hands sweating and throat closing. *I don't know if I can do this.* I drove to the hospital, praying on repeat, *Oh Jesus, please sustain me. Please don't let me faint. There's no way they'll send this kid home with me if I faint.*

I have good reason to think I may faint. I have a long and humiliating rap sheet of fainting at inopportune times. Like that time a friend's daughter had a seizure in the middle of Barnes & Noble, and I reacted the way any strong, capable mother would: fainting movie-style onto the floor in the middle of the store. It wasn't so bad until the people who had been helping the little girl having a seizure had to leave her side and tend to me. Thankfully, her parents just thought I was on the floor, prostrate in intercession. But I don't think the DCF workers and nurses would look on it so kindly if I did the same thing in the middle of the hospital floor.

I'm afraid that very thing may happen, though, as I meet with the nurses. They talk about a femur break—how it's the most painful bone break, how you never break your femur "by accident," how it's only ever broken through a significant accident or serious abuse. How someone did this to him—how *she* did this to him. My mind and my body reject the horror of it all, and I can feel myself losing control.

And then I see the little boy, the one I'm there to mother. He sits in a Radio Flyer wagon, his mode of transportation while his legs are confined frog-leg style in a harness that extends from his shoulders to his feet. Beautiful brown skin, pudgy cheeks that make me want to lean in and brush my fingers against them, eyes that dart around in wonder and in fear. The love of a mother provides the supernatural ability to lift cars and hold off passing out, and I'm strengthened by my immediate mother's love for him.

I bring him home and tend to his wounds and tend to his heart and step into the role of his mama. We fall into our new normal—until we receive the call that it's time to see *her*. I can't believe this child—broken-boned, brokenhearted—is going to be made to sit in a room with the woman who did this to him. I wasn't there to protect him when it happened, and I'm completely powerless to protect him from her again.

I drive him to his visit, pull him out of his car seat, and walk across the parking lot. I lock eyes with her. My mouth doesn't open, but I speak it to her loudly in my mind's voice: *You are my enemy.*

It's Never Easy

Sometimes rooting for my foster child's family is "easy." Like the young first-time mom who got into a bad relationship and just needs some support and a second chance. Like the dad who cries every time he sees his baby, who has a steady job and a place to live, and is stepping up for his child. Like the parents who are grateful and kind, working hard and fighting to change.

But really, even in these situations where my kids' parents are easy to support, I find it hard. Even then, my feelings toward them, my thoughts about them, aren't easily contained. It's hard to put myself in their shoes, to understand the story that's brought them to this place. It's hard to see the way their child has suffered and to think charitably still.

And believe me, I've had parents who are straight-up hard as well. Like the ones who slandered me on social media. (Don't judge; you Facebook stalk too.) Like the ones who called an investigation on me out of spite, who left me heartbroken and afraid and graced with a suspended license. Like the ones who've acted as if court was less about a child's life and more like a game to be won.

On a good day, I may use a Christianese phrase like "I'm struggling to love them." On a bad day, I just flat-out say it: "I hate them." Either way, I need some direction for this fight. How do I think and feel toward someone who has hurt a child I love, someone who has hurt me?

When it's too complicated to pull through the tangled threads of all my beliefs and emotions and expectations, I flip the script and simplify the struggle. I rename the discussion completely. I don't have to sort through each piece individually. Instead, I can label my kids' parents with a simple word, one that you would, most likely, never expect: *enemy*.

Love Your Enemies

See, God doesn't provide specific direction for the complicated biological–foster parent relationship in His Word. And I can't quite sort out how to feel about the mom who so clearly loves her child but makes choices like she loves meth just a little bit more. I don't know how to think about the mom who cries about how much she misses her son yet doesn't take advantage of the all-access daily visits she's allowed. I don't know how to feel about the mom who is beginning to make good choices but still ultimately chooses the sex offender over her daughter. It's all just too convoluted; I can't wrap my head around it.

But I know how to deal with my enemies. God speaks to that, loud and clear:

> "Love your enemies, do good to those who hate you, bless those who curse you, pray for those who mistreat you." (Luke 6:27–28 NIV)

> "Do not repay anyone evil for evil. . . . On the contrary: 'If your enemy is hungry, feed him; if he is thirsty, give him something to drink. In doing this, you will heap burning coals on his head.'" (Romans 12:17, 20 NIV)

> "Do not repay evil with evil or insult with insult. On the contrary, repay evil with blessing." (1 Peter 3:9 NIV)

> "Love your enemies and pray for those who persecute you." (Matthew 5:44)

I find "enemy" to be a helpful category because it includes, well, everyone. Whether I'm actually experiencing threats and accusations or "just" struggling through hurts and disappointments, I have the same answer: love, do good, bless, and so on. Even when I reduce my relationship with kids' parents down to the lowest common denominator, I still know how God commands me to think about them and treat them.

Love. Love doesn't have to be deserved, can't be earned. I don't love my kids' parents because they're particularly lovely. I love them because they were created by God and are loved by Him, because they have dignity as His image bearers and worth as His beloved. I also don't love my kids' parents because I feel an automatic and overwhelming sense of affection for them. Love isn't an emotion. It's an action. What good news this is for those of us who don't *feel* love but are committed to *doing* love.

> Love is patient, love is kind. It does not envy, it does not boast, it is not proud. It does not dishonor others, it is not self-seeking, it is not easily angered, it keeps no record of wrongs. Love does not delight in evil but rejoices with the truth. It always protects, always trusts, always hopes, always perseveres. (1 Corinthians 13:4–7 NIV)

Are these the beliefs and motivations that govern your relationship with your foster child's parents? What would it look like for you to love in a way that walks in patience? To love in a way that isn't self-seeking? To love in a way that keeps no record of wrongs?

Do good. We have the opportunity to serve those who may not "deserve" it, who may never thank us for it. Whether it's a Mother's Day card, an extra-specially packed visit bag, or a kind word, we can do good for our kids' parents. Sometimes this is a classic "fake it 'til you make it" action. You don't have to feel all the right things, you don't even have to *want* to do the good, but you can do good to your kids' parents out of love-motivated obedience.

Some of our children's parents have never experienced the type of no-strings-attached kindness we offer. My friend Lisa recounts when her sons' birth mom told her, "I've never had a relationship like this before. I've never had someone who wasn't trying to get something from me." Doing good looks like showing kindness without ulterior motives and without expectation. It walks out the unconditional love of Christ that we've experienced ourselves.

Bless. When cursed, we can use our words to bless. Bless your child's parents by speaking words of encouragement and life.[1] Let them know that you're praying for them, that you believe in them, that you hope they can be with their child soon. Say things that you believe, even if you don't feel them. It's not a lie for me to say, "I hope your child can be with you soon," to a mom struggling with heroin addiction, because I'm not saying, "I hope your child can come join you in your heroin flophouse and be neglected." I'm saying, "I hope you're freed from the oppression of addiction, that you are healed and able to see all that your child needs from you, and that you will grow into the person who can provide it so your child can be with you again soon." I've said to parents many things I don't *feel*, because I *believe* them and I'm praying that God helps me to feel them.

Pray. While I prayed bedtime prayers with my son last night, I prayed for a little girl at school whom I know he struggles with. "God, please help Wes to love and be kind to Lucy."

"Ugh, Lucy's the worst," he interjected midprayer. I choked down my laughter and—after five minutes of pleading—forced him to repeat the words, "God, I know that You love Lucy." It's all he could get out. Me? I'm a little bit like my son. Sometimes, I don't want to pray for my kids' parents. Sometimes I can barely speak their names. But if our God is a God who loves redemption, then our prayers should mirror His heart. We should pray loving prayers of healing and reconciliation and blessing and favor.

Repay. People talk about "payback." God tells us what payback looks like in His upside-down kingdom: *Repay evil with blessing.* You want payback? Repay their evil with blessing. Get your payback by blessing them.

A parent of one of my kids once called a child abuse referral on me because I sent expired baby food on a visit. I had literally bought the package of baby food *the day before.* I made an honest mistake, which I could have explained and apologized for if they had approached me rather than calling the child abuse hotline. When the worker called me to investigate, I was—how should I put it?—absolutely bubbling with rage.

"Well, it's not my responsibility to send food anyway, so how about I just stop sending it altogether?" was my simple solution. "They can go buy their own baby food and take some responsibility for providing for their kid for once." I was ready for payback. The worker gently chided me, and God gently convicted me. The next visit I sent *more* food, *extra* snacks (even something for the parents themselves), and a note explaining how sorry I was. I repaid with blessing.

Is there anything that drips of the gospel more than repaying evil with good? This is the ultimate trade-in that we experienced when Jesus died on the cross. He took our punishment—paid for our sin *against Him*—and traded it for His righteousness. Lavishly repaying the undeserving with blessing is the living, breathing gospel acted out before our kids' parents.

And isn't that what this is all about anyway? Because before being the one who shows mercy, I'm one who has received mercy. Before being the one who forgives, I'm the forgiven. Before being the one who loves my enemy, *I was the enemy.* "While we were enemies we were reconciled to God by the death of his Son" (Romans 5:10).

When I was God's enemy—not simply one who was wandering and lost but one who was railing against Him, one of the "haters of God" (Romans 1:30)—I was reconciled to Him. How? *By His Son.* He didn't just accept me as a friend; He made the way for me to no longer be His enemy.

The reason I label my children's parents as "enemy" is because it's then that I most clearly see how God wants me to treat them: the same way He treats His enemies. God doesn't tolerate or overlook His enemies, He doesn't even just forgive them. He brings them into relationship with Himself. He—the offended—makes the effort to create relationship, to pursue and restore. I don't know what you've been through with your foster children's parents, but I know that you have never been sinned against the way the holy Son of God has been sinned against. Perfect and sinless, He was murdered on a tree. And for the people who were murdering Him, He called out a prayer pleading for their forgiveness.

But What about Justice?

God's direction for dealing with our enemies is counterintuitive, countercultural, seemingly counterproductive. I'm the first one to get my back up and stand up for myself and others, and verses about "blessing" and "doing good" are like a slap in the face to my sense of justice and righteousness and, well, self-righteousness.

It's not fair that these people can hurt their children and play the system and threaten me, and I'm supposed to just . . . love? They need to be taught a lesson, or they'll never learn. They need to be shown what's what, or they'll just do it again.

The ability to love our enemies is found in a deep trust in our God. In our finiteness, we think that if we don't see and experience justice now, injustice must be reigning. But our God always reigns. He will right every wrong and repair every broken thing. He will punish wrongs and defeat evil. Sometimes He will even restore and redeem what we—in our limited wisdom—thought needed to be punished and defeated. In any case, God will have the final word with our enemies. In every case, He will reward our love to them.

Brokenness pulled us into these relationships in the first place, so it's no surprise when brokenness touches them still. Sometimes loving people who are so hard to love feels impossible.

But, friend, you were loved by God when you were hard to love. You are still. "Beloved, if God so loved us, we also ought to love one another" (1 John 4:11). When I'm weary and weak and unwilling, I remember this love—shown to an enemy—that has colored every part of my life. It is the love of Christ that made my dead heart alive and able to love and that gives me the strength to do all things, even love my foster child's family.[2]

eight

God Is in the Wait

I often feel like a sagacious old grandmother, spouting unwanted clichés to a soon-to-be or newbie foster parent: *"Oh, just be patient, dear, it will happen in its time."*

I know the truth now, that this journey takes patience, lots and lots of patience. But then, when I was first learning to wait, everything inside me railed against these words.

My wrestling with waiting began even before I had a foster child in my home. Once the passion for foster care blossomed in my heart, it wasn't going anywhere. Apparently, in a marriage, it's frowned upon to make a unilateral decision that affects the entire trajectory of your life without your spouse being on board, so there was that. But I couldn't sit still knowing there were kids who needed a home and that our home could be the one for them. So, I launched Operation Convince Alan to Become a Foster Parent.

First, I provided him with the most heartstring-pulling article I could find about foster care. "What did you think?" I asked expectantly. "Yeah, it's really sad," was his noncommittal answer.

Second, I printed photos of actual waiting foster children and taped them around the house, pretending they'd always been there. Third, I convinced him to read *Radical* by David Platt[1] and periodically dropped subtle questions like, "So, how do you think we're living sacrificially and radically out of love for Jesus and others?" I can't remember his exact answer, but I'm sure it included a laugh and an eye roll. Finally, I sat him down, looked him in the eyes, and said, "Babe. Listen, I feel burdened for this. I feel called to it. I'm asking you to really pray about it."

"Sign us up for the state's info session, and I promise you that I will pray," he replied. On December 24, as we exchanged our night-before-Christmas gifts, I unwrapped a note with a promise to pursue this dream: "Let's become foster parents," it read. I was ready—right that second—to have a child in my home. *Right that second.*

I had waited for my husband to get on board (which I've since learned is the universal experience of 99 percent of married foster moms). Then I waited for the first information meeting. I waited for our first home study appointment, our first training, our first inspection. I waited for the license, the first call, the first placement. I didn't do well through any of the waiting, holding my impatience with a stubborn grip. Nine months later—exactly as long as it takes to bring a child into your family the old-fashioned way—we welcomed our first foster daughter. Now I had a child to love on. The wait was over.

Except that it wasn't. Once the wait to become foster parents ended, the real waiting began. We waited for the first bit of information, the first court date, the first ruling. We waited for parents to show up to visits and psychologists to give their expert opinions. We waited for reunification timelines and adoption days. The wait continued and continues still.

It was hard, but it's gotten easier. Patience has become a learned friend.

A People Always Waiting

Waiting isn't just a foster parent thing. It's a Christian thing. Being a child of God is defined by waiting. Since God's promise in the garden, His people have waited for all things to be made new. They waited for the promised land, and they waited for the arrival of the Messiah. We wait for our promised land of heaven still and for the Messiah to return. Waiting is a part of the Christian DNA. Since Adam and Eve pulled our human race into brokenness, we've lived in perpetual waiting for things to become again as they were first created to be.

My favorite biblical example of waiting—or maybe even of how *not* to wait—is my biblical hero, Abraham. I'm a big fan of Abraham. I'm inspired by the tale of sacrifice and faith, and I relate to the tale of doubt and fear and, well, stupidity. I considered—for about a millisecond—naming my first son after him, until I realized that it would mean my kid would forever be stuck with the name Abraham (my deepest apologies if your son's name is Abraham). Let's talk about my friend Abraham's experience of waiting.

Though the reality of infertility is very real to many in the foster care community—and there is a strong theme of trusting God through infertility—this story has lessons beyond that for all of us who have been called to a period of waiting. The story begins with God calling Abraham (at the time, known as Abram) from his home to a different country, a place where God would make him into a great nation.[2] Abram follows God, "even though he did not know where he was going" (Hebrews 11:8 NIV), and God promises both to bless Abram and that

Abram will "be a blessing" (Genesis 12:2). But the key to this promise centers around the very first step needed for the promise to be fulfilled: a son. For an entire nation to be birthed from you, you need at least one child, and Abram and his wife, Sarai (later known as Sarah), had already experienced about fifty years of infertility.

Abram and Sarai doubted God throughout the journey. Can you say, "No, Abram, I'm your wife, and I will not say I'm your sister and join that man's harem to save your life"? *Two different times.*[3] Or what about the time they decided that God was taking too long, and they took matters into their own hands and offered up Sarai's servant, Hagar, as Abram's sleeping buddy and the baby mama of the promised heir?[4] Or how about when *God Himself* appeared to Abram to remind him of the promise, and both Abram and Sarai laughed at the idea of having a child in their old age?[5]

Eventually, God brought them their child "at the very time God had promised him" (Genesis 21:2 NIV)—a good twenty-four years after the initial promise, most likely decades later than Abram and Sarai wanted or expected, and right at God's absolutely perfect timing. They had their son. Abraham was a father and would go on to become the father of many nations and the father of God's chosen people. The rest, as they say, is Old Testament biblical history.

Though Abraham and Sarah appear as the main characters, they aren't the most important players in this story, and they're not the source of where the real lesson lies.[6] Abraham and Sarah weren't exactly model "waiters" (considering the laughing and the doubting and the sleeping with maidservants and all). But God knew how they would fail, and *He chose them anyway.* Just think: He could have chosen someone who would walk with more strength and wherewithal for the task, but He didn't.

He could have selected the most patient human He had ever created, but He didn't. He could have made this promise to a baby-making machine, but He didn't. He could have eliminated the wait altogether. *But He didn't.*

The lessons within Abraham and Sarah's waiting for their promised son have very little to do with how Abraham and Sarah actually waited and everything to do with the God who was orchestrating everything behind the scenes of the wait. It always has less to do with us and more to do with Him, doesn't it? The lesson: You will fail. You will be impatient. You will operate in fear. But God will accomplish His perfect plan in His perfect timing, despite you.

If you are a foster parent, you will learn patience. You can learn it by practicing the Finn kids' definition of patience by "waiting with a happy heart." Or you can learn it by kicking and screaming and complaining and worrying. But you *will* learn it just the same.

Maybe you're waiting for your license or your first placement. Maybe you're waiting for a court date or a ruling. Maybe you're waiting for information about your reunified foster child or that long-yearned-for adoption date. Maybe you're waiting for your child's heart to turn around or behavior to change. God is there with you in the wait in countless ways, and in four ways specifically.

1. The Wait Is Part of the Story

Waiting isn't a preface or precursor. As much as the wait may feel merely like the "before" that precedes the real thing, it is very much a part of the actual story.

I look to the example of my friend Mel in this. She and her husband are missionaries—in identity and in calling, even if not yet in action. They felt the call to be missionaries to Mexico, were accepted by a missions organization, completed their fundraising . . . and accepted the placement of a little girl who was a "sure, quick adoption." *Collective sigh.* You know how that one goes. They've spent the past three years in a holding pattern, waiting for their little girl's appeal process to be settled. Unable to leave for their mission field until their daughter is adopted, unable to fully settle here with the mission field still calling, they live in the in-between.

But they don't *just* live in the in-between. They live very presently where they are right here, right now. They serve in their church and in their community, they build relationships and form plans, they live with joy and purpose. They even had a surprise adoption that wouldn't have happened without being "stuck" in New Jersey, which Mel acknowledges as an obvious part of an otherwise unclear plan. They have experienced the joy of being *here*, even as they've waited to be *there*. Mel eagerly preaches the beauty of the wait whenever she's given the chance. "The truths found on every cliché Hobby Lobby sign are what's gotten me through it," she says. "The wait is part of the story. The waiting room is part of the journey. It's not just about passing through; it's a part of the joy and a part of the lesson."

Waiting can feel like the most passive human experience, but our times of waiting shouldn't be wasted finger tapping and watch checking. Godly waiting is active. Even when there's a waiting period in one area of our lives, there's something to be done somewhere else. Even as we anticipate what will come tomorrow, we have a mission to fulfill today.

2. God Is Working Out the Details in His Timing

I remember when I read my daughter's file and saw all the hotline referral calls that came and were ignored before she joined our family, all the times she "should have" been removed and wasn't. I felt physically ill. Someone dropped the ball. Someone didn't protect this child. But then I noticed the dates and this reality: If she had been removed the first time a call was placed, it would have been before I was even a foster parent. She would not have been placed in my home. She wouldn't be my daughter. She'd be someone else's daughter. Do I wish she had been removed the first time? Of course. Do I trust the God who ordained for her to be placed in our family? Absolutely. I have countless friends with stories like this. Stories of unmet expectations and failed timelines and broken plans that God used to accomplish His exactly right plan.

Maybe you'll learn details like this that calm your impatient heart. Chances are you won't. Either way, God is perfectly arranging the details of your life and your children's lives in His perfect timing.[7]

3. You'll Learn Lessons the Only Way They Can Be Learned

"She's pulling out a VHS! Oh my gosh, she's pulling out a VHS! I haven't seen one of those things in decades," Alan too loudly whispered, elbowing me with a laugh. We were sitting in session one of our twenty-four hours of DCF-required training. As if going through a textbook with a twentysomething trainer who wasn't even a parent didn't already seem insufficient to prepare us for foster parenting, we were now watching a made-in-1984 VHS tape.

Most of us walk into foster parenting undereducated and ill-equipped. But even if we're adequately trained, we could never be fully prepared for what we'll face. Some lessons can be learned only by being earned. Some character can be gained only through the difficult work of waiting.

You are learning something right now, growing into something right now. If you are God's child, He promises it. As you wait, the Holy Spirit is transforming you into Christ's likeness with ever-increasing glory.[8] As you wait, He is pruning you to become even more fruitful.[9] As you wait, He is carrying on His good work in you to completion.[10] You could never know what tools or traits you'll need for the next step of your foster parenting journey. But God knows exactly and is growing them in you. Right now, in your wait, you are becoming who you need to be to do what God has called you to do.

4. God Writes the Timeline

Mary, the mother of Jesus, was probably about fourteen when she became pregnant. Elizabeth, her cousin and the mother of John the Baptist, was "well advanced in years" (polite Bible talk for *really old*, maybe seventy). Fourteen and seventy are both arguably unideal ages to have a baby. Imagining these two women meeting as pregnant cousins makes me laugh. Mary, impregnated by God Himself. Elizabeth, with her aging body and aching joints, and the wild baby John leaping in her belly. Maybe they questioned their untimely pregnancies. Wouldn't they both have been better off if this had happened for each of them at, say, twenty? We, of course, have the benefit of hindsight. John and Jesus were perfectly, divinely ordained to be born around the same time, to be peers, to be partners in ministry. John had the important job of preparing the way of the Lord. Jesus was publicly revealed as the Son of God through John's ministry. These men "should" have been born fifty years apart. But God knew what He was doing.

Timelines work differently for the eternal God than they do for those of us whose lives are "like a breath" (Psalm 144:4). Reconciling our own experience of time with God's transcendence over it can be frustrating, but "the Lord is not slow in keeping his promise, as some understand slowness" (2 Peter 3:9 NIV).

Yes, God is the God of eternity past and future, for whom time doesn't define or limit, for whom a thousand years is like a day and a day like a thousand years.[11] But He's also the God who lifts and sets the sun to form our days, who appoints the day of salvation, who created a time and a season for everything under the sun.[12] God is intimately involved in your story and your children's stories and holds your times in His hands.[13] He makes "everything beautiful in its time" (Ecclesiastes 3:11), and He's beautifully writing the timeline of your life and your children's lives.

Still Learning

Three years into enduring the constant halts and delays of foster care, I concluded that I'd pretty much learned to wait well. I'd put in my ten thousand hours, earned my patch, so to speak. Foster care had put us through the wringer of waiting, but I decided that I had finally arrived at that oh so elusive destination of patience. And now we were only weeks away from the adoption of our daughters.

One of our girls' workers called. Her voice was vacant: "I didn't get the paperwork in on time." My stomach didn't just drop. It dropped and then flipped and then made its way up to stick in my throat. We had lost our adoption date. After all the waiting, after stretching our fingers to the finish line, so close we could nearly touch it, it was stripped away. Of course we would still eventually adopt our daughters. Of course this delay didn't actually change anything. But that almost made it worse. The waiting felt pointless, like waiting for waiting's sake.

The weariness of three years of waiting flooded my heart. I cried both out loud and in my heart something to the tune of

I can't do this. We had waited for timelines and parents and workers and judges, and now what were we even waiting for? "And now, O Lord, for what do I wait? *My hope is in you*" (Psalm 39:7, emphasis mine). The object of our waiting is a *Person.* We wait for the Lord. We don't wait for things to randomly unfold; we wait for our God to reveal what He has planned. And our discouragement can be transformed into sweet anticipation and eager expectation as we remember just Whom we are waiting for. "Wait for the LORD; be strong and take heart and wait for the LORD" (Psalm 27:14 NIV). I was worn down and weak, but strength was available in simply waiting on Him. He provided strength not just *for* the wait but also *in* the wait. Miraculous, otherworldly, divinely infused strength. "They who wait for the LORD shall renew their strength; they shall mount up with wings like eagles; they shall run and not be weary; they shall walk and not faint" (Isaiah 40:31).

nine

I Thought My Love Would Be Enough

One of the final steps in the adoption process that my husband and I went through, what the New Jersey child welfare system calls the "bonding evaluation," goes like this: The prospective adoptive parents and the hopefully soon-to-be-adopted child sit in a seven-by-seven-foot room with a table and four chairs, no toys, and a strange doctor with a notebook. Said doctor coldly directs, "Now interact with the child," watches and takes notes, judges the parents' bond with the child, and writes a report to the court that serves as a final recommendation for or against adoption. This "bonding eval" may more aptly be called "living nightmare."

Following our living nightmare was a more comfortable meeting with the doctor who performed the evaluation. My husband and I sat across from her, and the cold facade we faced during the evaluation had melted. She told us that her recommendation would be for adoption. That our bond with the child was beautiful, our relationship with her everything that a parent-child relationship should be. And then she shared about our soon-to-be-child's history. She spoke of mental health diagnoses and criminal records, of abuse and trauma, of broken people and broken family. As overwhelming fear clenched my heart, she leaned in with a reassuring smile and said, "But don't worry. Your love will heal her."

Oh my. This was just exactly what my heart wanted to hear. *My love is enough. She'll be a part of our happy family and never want to know anything else. It won't matter who she was born to or what happened to her. She'll experience our love, and then, oh, she'll come to know the love of God, and all will be made right.* This doctor's "prognosis" gave me hope. Everything was going to be okay. My love would make it okay.

A judge then slammed a gavel and called us a family. Life went on for a few months with the "my love will heal her" hope prognosis charging my days. And then one day, in a part of the story that isn't mine to tell, this illusion came crashing down. With painful clarity, I saw how my love *couldn't* make everything better—it couldn't remove her memories, it couldn't assuage her fear, it couldn't heal her body or brain or heart. It didn't matter how much I loved this child, my love was powerless to heal her.

What a rude awakening to a very true reality: my kids have experienced trauma, and it's not within my power to make everything okay for them.

This Isn't That Book

I'm no doctor, but if I were, I probably would have steered away from this doctor's "your love will heal" prescription and spoken more about a "complex developmental trauma" diagnosis. But, like I said, I'm not a doctor. I am, however, a lay theologian—simply put, someone who has thoughts about God—as are you, and theologically speaking, trauma can be described as the curse in action. It's what happens when our bodies react to suffering that they weren't created to experience. It changes the way the brain is wired, changes the chemistry of the body, changes the feelings and thoughts and behaviors of the one who endured it. Trauma is the effect of fallen bodies experiencing the damaging effects of suffering.

As foster parents, we care for children with broken stories, difficult pasts, and bodies and brains and hearts that continue to carry the damage of those things. Every one of our foster children has been touched by trauma—many of them unspeakable hardship and abuse, most of them significant neglect, all of them the loss of family. That perfect little baby you brought home from the hospital may have experienced within the womb the heightened cortisol levels related to domestic violence or the poisonous damage of alcohol. The little girl who is acting out could be operating out of the same survival skills that protected her in an abusive home, or she could be managing her trauma-induced sensory needs. The child who appears perfectly healthy and happy and quick to please may be dealing with unseen wounds and silent struggles.

As I admitted before, I am not a doctor. I am not an expert. This is not "that" book. If you're looking for that book, good! Go read that book![1] You need that book, your kids need you to read that book. But this is not that book. Rather, this book is like a conversation with someone who has walked the same path—who is stumbling along that path presently—and learned some lessons on the way.

Our families face things outside the scope of your average, run-of-the-mill parenting problems. Therefore, the ways you parent kids from hard places may look very different from the methods of the friends and family you're parenting alongside. They may even look different from the ways you're parenting your other children. But this book isn't about methods; it's about lessons.

The Lessons

Don't Worry about What Others Think

Sometimes we pick our battles and overlook an incident when another parent would dig in their heels. Sometimes we comfort instead of correct. Sometimes we make decisions contrary to the ones of those around us, maybe even decisions we never thought we'd make. No, we don't push away and ignore the voices of others—understanding that "in an abundance of counselors there is safety" (Proverbs 11:14)—but we carefully choose the voices of those who know our children, understand their needs and the pervasive effects of trauma, and can provide informed, knowledgeable counsel.

We vacation with my extended family each year. They are extremely compassionate and understanding toward our kids' needs, but family vacation has served as a crash course for me in parenting to the needs of my child and not falling into comparison or worrying about others' opinions. My kids' needs can be overwhelming and end up commanding the direction of our days. One of my children has a sensory processing disorder, which means the feeling of sand and sunblock and a wet bathing suit is a land mine of anxiety triggers. When this child starts complaining about sand in their bathing suit, we pack up and head home from the beach, even if everyone else just arrived. To an outsider, this may look like we're letting our kid's whims control our entire family, but we know that we're loving and protecting our child (not to mention, everyone else). The past neglect of one of my children means that social situations can be challenging for them. They can come across as antisocial or even unkind, but we don't force them to join the rest of the kids and participate and "be a good sport." We make a place on our lap and say, "Let's watch together."

It's interesting how our perception of what others think can be vastly different from what they're actually thinking. "We may not have always fully understood, but watching you parent the kids has helped us to grow in understanding trauma and the needs of those who've walked through it," my mom shared with me. "I am amazed how patient and consistent you and Alan are in your parenting," said my dad. "Short of God's grace, I don't see how you (or any other foster parents) handle your kids' struggles daily with the love and commitment you show." Here I was, feeling insecure and worrying about how other people were seeing us, and what they were actually seeing was an example. Our little family was serving to teach the people around us about trauma and even pointing them to the grace of God.

No matter what, our concern about what others may be thinking of our parenting cannot determine the way we parent. Our concern should always be for the good of our children and a desire to honor the Lord. "For am I now seeking the approval of man, or of God? Or am I trying to please man?" (Galatians 1:10).

Adjust and Readjust with Prayer

Changing your parenting strategies to meet your children right where they are each day is not being inconsistent, because your children's behavior probably won't be consistent from day to day. Becoming a trauma-informed parent means becoming a detective. It means looking past your child's behavior to their needs.

The best way I can detect what my children need—and how I can provide it—is to be in prayer, asking that God will show me. "If any of you lacks wisdom, you should ask God, who gives generously to all without finding fault, and it will be given to you" (James 1:5 NIV). When one of my kids began to have significant behavioral issues, we made the decision to dig in our heels and adopt a no-nonsense method of parenting. We would crack down on every yell, every throw, every hit until we "fixed" this kid. But our brilliant idea of consistent strictness didn't work. I cried out to God for direction and felt one simple word: *anxiety*. I began to see each of this child's behaviors through a lens of anxiety. This kid wasn't just angry and violent and mean. They were struggling and scared and anxious. They didn't need us to come at them because they weren't *acting* right; they needed us to come alongside them because they weren't *feeling* right.

I find it so comforting that Jesus told His disciples it was even better that He leave so that He could send the Holy Spirit to them.[2] I like to think that I'd always know exactly what to do if Jesus was by my side through life (you know, WWJD and all that), but Jesus Himself said that we're better off with the Holy Spirit inside us than with Him by our side. Maybe you will pray and "your ears will hear a voice behind you, saying, 'This is the way; walk in it'" (Isaiah 30:21 NIV). I rarely, if ever, experience the direction of the Lord like that. My experience looks more like praying and reading God's Word and getting a sense of peace in how I should proceed. It looks like crying out in the middle of something hard and being reminded of a convicting or comforting Scripture. It looks like praying for direction, love, and help, and experiencing His supernatural provision of it. God's direction may sound like a voice from heaven or a quiet whisper into your heart, but when you come to the Lord for direction and help, you can be confident that "the LORD will guide you always" (Isaiah 58:11 NIV).

Slow Down

I'm naturally a "You're fine; brush it off" kind of mom. I don't like drama, and I have too many people to be everything to everyone all the time. But I'm learning to slow down. To "be completely humble and gentle; [to] be patient, bearing with [others] in love" (Ephesians 4:2 NIV), to nurture, to be my kids' safe place for comfort. I'm learning to meet not just the physical and spiritual and mental but also the emotional.

One child I cared for needed to be reassured of the details of a plan over and over and over to feel comfortable. It made me want to pull out my hair, but it helped them to feel safe, so I went over the plan again and again and again. Another of my foster children needed every physical or emotional hurt to be acknowledged and comforted, or they would carry it through the rest of the day and into the night, so I gave hugs and wiped tears and distributed unnecessary Band-Aids.

Many of the kids who come to us through foster care missed out on those crucial first months of met needs, of a responsive mama, of learning "When I cry, someone comes." And so it's up to us to redo what was left undone. To "baby" the child who wasn't babied, to step in with comfort and nurture, and to make sure they know—in their hearts, bodies, and brains—that they are safe and loved.

It's Not Me; It's You

Please tell me you've heard the words, "You're not my real mom" or "I hate you." I'm sorry to wish ill will on anyone, but

I just need to know I'm not alone here. One of my kids is so incredibly inventive and intelligent in their insults, it's almost amusing. "I wish your mom and your dad never met so that they didn't get married, so that you weren't born and never became my mom." I waver between crying from the hurt and congratulating them on a solid burn.

My kids' struggles are just that: *their* struggles. But when I'm the one they look to for help, and when I—holding the privileged title of "safe place"—get the brunt of it all, it can be hard to remember that.

This is an issue of identity. I don't know what the voice of God sounds like, but I imagine it sounds a whole lot like James Earl Jones. I can hear the booming voice of JEJ as King Mufasa saying to his child, Simba—or, metaphorically speaking, the King speaking to His child, me—"Remember who you are." (Sue me, I love *The Lion King*.) If I see myself primarily as a forgiven child of God,[3] then I don't define my success as a parent based on my kids' definition of my success. Maybe my children see and point out my weakness. Yep, it's there, all right. But it's forgiven, and I bear the weight of it no more. It is not what I do, how well I'm doing it, or my children's evaluations of how well I'm doing it that brings me worth or value. The accusatory claims of my kids can't shake me because I remember who I am before God.

Love and Accept My Kids as They Are

I've had to learn to really love and accept my kids, despite *and because of* their personalities, diagnoses, stories, and weaknesses. There are things about my kids that, to be brutally honest, I just don't like. I wish this one would smile and answer when someone asks a question. I wish this one wouldn't bounce off the walls like a wild animal. I wish this one would ever, just once, talk before crying.

Accepting kids as they are sometimes means moving the line for success. I celebrate smaller victories and show more grace and readjust my expectations. It most certainly means reminding myself that my children are "fearfully and wonderfully made" (Psalm 139:14), "[God's] workmanship, created in Christ Jesus" (Ephesians 2:10). They are precious to Him and precious to me. But sometimes I have to do the work of reorienting my heart to their preciousness, reminding myself of the love that I do, in fact, have for them. When my kids have particularly difficult days, my husband and I visit each of their bedrooms while they sleep. We look at their little faces. We comment on how one's arm is carelessly thrown over their head, how one's bottom always sticks in the air while they sleep, how one's lips form a pucker. We predictably say something like, "They're so cute," and my eyes inevitably fill with tears. Sometimes I am naturally overwhelmed by feelings of love for my children, but sometimes I have to do the work of putting on love.[4]

Lie under the Bed with Those Who Lie under the Bed

Every wife needs a husband like Alan Finn. About a year ago, Alan took over the household laundry, and my family experienced an incredibly unique laundry problem. You see, my husband's laundry game was so on point that the outfits the kids wore the day before would be neatly folded and waiting for them on their dressers the next day. Left to their own devices, they would wear the same clean outfit day after day, on and on, forever. How many households have *this* problem? He has all the ingredients of the perfect 1950s "housewife," but he also has those nurturing, maternal qualities of a great mom. The kids are much more prone to wake him in the middle of the night than they are me, and they're all more likely to cry in his arms than they are in mine.

I'll never forget the day I walked into my foster child's room and saw Alan lying on the floor, face to the ground, reaching under the bed silently. This child had a tendency to hide when afraid or otherwise "triggered." We found her in closets and corners of dark bathrooms and sometimes under beds. While I might be tempted to march in, pull her out from under the bed, and try to talk out her problem with all my fix-it-ness, my husband knew what she needed: presence. A hand outstretched, eyes locked, another soul to sit with her in her sadness. She needed the silent comfort of togetherness, the consolation of company. This love from her father mirrored *the* Father's love, from which nothing can separate us.[5] Her father's presence mirrored *the* Father's presence: no matter where we hide, we find He is there.[6]

I want to fly in, in all my Supermom glory, and make things right, but my cape only tangles me up. Sometimes the best way to love our kids is to sit—or lie, face to the ground—with them in their sadness. "Weep with those who weep" (Romans 12:15). "Mourn with those who mourn" (NIV). And lie under the bed with those who lie under the bed. We can't fix our children's struggles, change their stories, answer all their questions. We can't take away our children's griefs, but we can enter them and stay with our children there.

God Our Healer

The same God who healed the snakebites of the Israelites, who took on human form and made the blind see, the lame walk, and the bleeding clean, is the same God we follow today. Our God, "who heals all your diseases" (Psalm 103:3), is able to rewire our children's brains, recalibrate their brain chemistries, regenerate their nervous systems, mend their wounds, *heal their bodies*.

Our God, who, as the Holy Spirit, is named "Comforter" (John 15:26 KJV), who "heals the brokenhearted and binds up their wounds" (Psalm 147:3), can *heal their hearts*. We come to Jesus like the man in Mark 9, with our children in our arms, hopeful but struggling with faith:

> "If you can do anything, take pity on us and help us."
> "'If you can'?" said Jesus. "Everything is possible for one who believes." (vv. 22–23 NIV)

Our God is able to heal, and He calls us to pray and believe He can. I don't know about you, but I say along with the father in this passage, "I believe; help my unbelief!" (v. 24).

Traditional Christian Parenting versus Trauma-Informed Parenting

As I've learned more about trauma and the brain, I've had to wrestle with the traditional Christian parenting that I'd always subscribed to.

Disobedience *is* a sin. Stealing *is* wrong. Violence *is not* okay. But if I ascribe *only* sinful motives to my kids' "wrong" behavior—and ignore the trauma history or physiological components of their struggles—then I'm only seeing part of the picture. When I tell my child to put on their clothes for school and they refuse because the tag on the shirt "hurts," I can't just dig in my heels and demand compliance. I have to remember that sensory processing disorder and obsessive-compulsive disorder are debilitating forces that my child battles. When my child hoards food and hides it in the corner under their bed, I can't be shocked and punish them for "stealing." I have to remember that the effects of food insecurity and neglect on their brain and body continue to guide them into survival mode, even though they have access to all the food they need. When my child tailspins into a screaming and kicking rage because their toy breaks, they're not simply lacking self-control. The drugs, alcohol, and stress they were exposed to in utero left them with brain damage and increased cortisol levels that affect their ability to regulate their emotions.

So through which lens should I view my child? Are my kids inherently sinful, needing forgiveness? Or are they sufferers of trauma, living with brains and bodies that have been affected by what they've experienced? The answer isn't either/or. It is both/and. As a Christian foster parent, I need to see my children as in need of both the forgiveness of Jesus for their souls and the physical healing of their bodies and brains.

Our children are broken because they've experienced abuse and neglect and suffered the loss of biological family. Our children are broken because they've experienced the devastating effects of another's brokenness. *But that's not all.* Our children are broken for the same reason we are broken: because they're humans who need God. We cannot become so focused on raising successful, well-adjusted children with healthy attachments that we lose sight of the fact that our children are lost souls who need to be made right with God. Our children have many needs, but first and foremost is the need we share with them: the need for Jesus.

When We're the Problem

My kids aren't the biggest problem in my house. I am.[7] I am impatient and unkind, selfish and lazy, easily offended and easily angered, hopeless and fearful. This isn't a "None of us are perfect, so feel better about yourself" kind of list. Each of these sins plagues me, affects my children, and deserves the punishment of God.

Thank the Lord, He has provided a way for forgiveness and transformation. When He forgave me, He didn't just wipe my slate clean; He declared me righteous and began the process of helping me live righteously.[8] This is called "sanctification," and it's something we work on together. I take my heart to task, doing the work of confession and repentance and growth. But I can do those things only through the power and strength God provides. I love reading the "He and I" dynamic side by side in Colossians 1:29: "For this *I* toil, struggling with all *his* energy that *he* powerfully works within me" (emphasis mine).

And still I fail. I so want to do this foster care thing well, and then every day my weakness touches it all. But the weakness is actually a gift, leading me to hope for myself and for my kids. My hope is in Jesus, to empower me to be what my kids need, to forgive me when I'm not, to help them in all the places I can't. I need the saving grace of my Father for my failures, just as my kids need it for theirs. The good news is that this is something I can always give them. When I'm the strong glue holding us all together, we need Him, and I can speak of Him and live a life that reflects Him. And when I'm the weak link, crumpled at the center of our family mess, I can point to Him as the One who forgives us while we're still down and gives the grace to pull us out of it.

I'll never forget when I got to hear one of my favorite authors and speakers, Ann Voskamp, teach at a conference for foster and adoptive parents. I had spent the day in breakouts about trauma and sensory needs and education plans, and I sat down in the session feeling overwhelmed by all that I had to do to help my children heal. Ann began speaking and sharing about her own broken story and then her adopted daughter's broken heart (literally, her daughter was born with a hole in her heart). She acknowledged the temptation for us, as parents who so deeply love our children, to want to put together our children's broken pieces and make everything all right for them. In a powerful moment, she threw out her arms and gathered up the imagined broken pieces and then turned to the cross that hung on the back wall of the church. "Our job," she said, "is simply to gather up those broken pieces and place them at the foot of the cross."[9]

My temptation is to waver between hopelessness and saviorism. Many days I fall somewhere in between raising my hands in defeat and taking up my children's healing like it all depends on me.

Our God asks for faithfulness. For love. For sacrificial service. He doesn't ask us to produce anything, change anything, or heal anything, and it's not our job to save. When we embrace that we are powerless to heal, we are able to play a part in the healing. And when we acknowledge that we are not saviors, we can step into our children's stories and walk with them and lead them to the Savior.

ten

What Do You Have That You Did Not Receive?

eplorable housing" was the documented reason for removal. *Come on. I don't like to clean, either, but this is so simple. Just clean your house and get your kid back. Don't you even care?*

The caseworker sat on my couch, opened the file, and wove a tale that broadened my view past Mom's messy house and inside Mom's messy life. Mom's own mother struggled with addiction and eventually killed herself, but the fallout kept coming. A life of poverty. A father who was not present. A sister with significant developmental delays. A chronic, life-threatening illness. A string of men who abused and used and hurt her.

I felt it in my bones. The deep conviction of an arrogant, self-righteous heart. The extraordinary gift of an extraordinarily privileged life. "What do you have that you did not receive?" (1 Corinthians 4:7) came like an audible voice that pierced my heart and changed my life.

My entire life has been defined by love. My parents were—still are—devoted first to Jesus, then to each other, then to me and my brothers. My dad taught me to dream big dreams for Jesus, to do absolutely anything for my family, and to love the Beatles. My mom taught me that words bring life and encouragement, that a wife and mom can be devoted to serving those both inside and outside of her home. My brothers were—still are—my best friends, and we share countless happy memories of childhood together. I have never wanted for anything, never been hurt by anyone. I've only experienced love, only known kindness.

My life was marked by stability, privilege, and opportunity. How dare I look at the broken life of this broken woman with anything but compassion?

What about You?

What about your life? Does the flickering film of your childhood mirror my own happy and safe story? Are your memories of love and kindness and joy? Maybe you need the same rebuke I needed: *You've been given a life of love and privilege and happiness. How dare you judge! What do you have that you did not receive?*

Or maybe your story is more like that of my foster daughter's mother: abuse, addiction, loss, instability, illness, hopelessness. Maybe it's easy for you to point a finger because you survived the same and pulled yourself out of it.

Friend, I say to you still: *What do you have that you did not receive?* If God has given you the strength or resilience, resources or support to rise above your circumstances—to beat the odds of your childhood, to be a great parent even when you didn't have a great parent, to battle and win the fight against addiction, to overcome—then all the more so: *What do you have that you did not receive?* I don't know your kids' parents' stories. I don't know what they've put their kids through, what they've put you through. But I know this: your kids' parents are just as deserving of grace as you are. Which is *not at all*. But aren't you glad you've received it just the same?

May our stories—no matter what they tell—never lead to anything but great humility and gratitude. May the cry of our hearts only and ever be, "By the grace of God I am what I am" (1 Corinthians 15:10).

To Whom Much Is Given . . .

This morning I woke in a safe and warm bed. I took a hot shower and sorted through my large closetful of clothes. I drank a cup of coffee and ate a healthy breakfast. I kissed my husband goodbye and drove my kids to school. I worked at a job I love and came home to a family I enjoy. I experienced "grace upon grace" (John 1:16).

But my life is also very hard. It's full of very challenging children and very stressful work and a very demanding schedule. And to be honest, it's much easier to see the hard and be filled with anxiety and complaint than it is to see the blessings and be filled with gratitude. My heart rarely drifts into gratitude. More often I'm making a choice to search out and find the gifts, engaging in a fight to see how what I receive is actually good and perfect.

We are incessant gift receivers—of the gift of life, the gift of faith, the gifts of every person and relationship and bite of food and item of clothing. Every piece of our lives is an undeserved present from a loving Father. "Every good and perfect gift is from above" (James 1:17 NIV).

When we become convinced that everything we have is something we've received, that concept changes us. Now, rather than being "something" in our own minds, we see that we are actually "nothings" who have been gifted *everything*. That revelation increases our humility. It multiplies our compassion. It brings the understanding that nothing we've experienced or become or overcome really has anything at all to do with us. It changes the way we view others—particularly our foster children's parents. It shifts everything. We become so focused on what we've been given that we become obsessive givers. To whom much is given, much is required,[1] and we have been given so much. Rich, poor, married, single, healthy, sick, with baggage or none, you are walking through life with your arms full of extravagant gifts. You can hoard these gifts and be weighed down by their load, or you can view them as borrowed resources, given *to* you only to be given *by* you again. As foster parents, we are surrounded by people who are in need of the gifts we carry.

The shift I experienced through my "What do you have that you did not receive?" epiphany changed the way I saw and thought about my foster daughter's mother, but it also changed the way I treated her. I began offering her undeserved gifts the same way I'd received undeserved gifts.

My perspective changed from "What do I *have* to do?" to "What do I *get* to do?" Yes, I *have* to send her daughter to visits with her. But I *get* to send her to the visits wearing her Halloween costume and Christmas dress. I *get* to write back and forth in a journal and chat through email and text. I *get* to invite her to doctors' appointments and evaluations. I *get* to have a special birthday party just for biological family and friends.

As someone who has been given much, I get to give much.

Justice Warriors

Foster parents are like a guerrilla army of justice warriors. We see suffering and sadness and injustice, and we are compelled to act. We infiltrate a broken system and fight for change and battle in love. We "speak up for those who cannot speak for themselves" (Proverbs 31:8 NIV); we "correct oppression"; we "bring justice to the fatherless" (Isaiah 1:17).

Our hearts mirror our God's heart when we love justice. He is a just God, and He has placed in our hearts a drive for things to be made right and for justice to rise victorious. But our hearts also mirror God's when we love mercy. He is a merciful God, and He has placed in our hearts an empathetic love that sees brokenness and is driven to step into it with compassion.

God's justice is like the black velvet cloth that magnifies the glistening diamond of His mercy. Justice and mercy are brought to perfection in relationship to each other. As His followers, may we not seek justice without also loving mercy.[2]

My kids love to talk about what's fair when it benefits them. *She gets to go to bed after me? That's not fair! He gets to choose the show again? That's not fair!* But most of the "unfairness" in our home plays out very differently. Like "You only have to eat one piece of broccoli, and then you can have a cookie" kind of unfair. Like "I know we said you'll have an early bedtime, but let's watch a family movie instead" kind of unfair. My kids receive undeserved, unearned gifts and mercies every day. It's not fair.

Thank the Lord that life isn't fair. The most unfair thing I've ever experienced? The extravagant love I received from my God. Fair would be *me* on the cross, being punished for my own sins. Fair would be getting a clean slate and one chance not to screw it up again rather than the daily, minute-by-minute forgiveness and restoration I receive. Fair would be separation from God and misery and hell. But God is a God who "is kind to the ungrateful and the evil" (Luke 6:35). I live an unfair life, and God calls me to share this same unfair love.

Jesus taught, "If someone slaps you on one cheek, turn to them the other also. If someone takes your coat, do not withhold your shirt from them. Give to everyone who asks you, and if anyone takes what belongs to you, do not demand it back" (Luke 6:29–30 NIV). Let's be clear. If you were to slap me, I wouldn't just take it. If you were to take something that belongs to me, I would absolutely demand it back. Was Jesus calling His disciples to become willing victims of abuse and theft? Of course not. Was He calling them to become radical, self-sacrificing lovers who care more about others than their own rights? Absolutely. Jesus calls us to a love that is so generous, so over-the-top lavish, that it's actually unfair.

Regarding the moms of most of my kids, I can come up with approximately four hundred reasons why they don't deserve, for example, a Mother's Day gift. But I can come up with two very good reasons that trump them and push me to buy one anyway. First, God divinely and without mistake endowed her with a role that is worthy of honor, even if her behavior isn't. Second, there are four thousand reasons that I don't deserve all the things I've received, yet God has loved me with a profuse and unfair kind of love. And He calls me to be merciful, even as He is merciful.[3]

May we give our coats and our shirts and our unslapped cheeks to our kids' parents through kind words and thoughtful gifts and support and love.

I Run Out of Tampons Too

I texted my girlfriend group chat.

> Me:
> Tommy's mom just asked for $100 for tampons.
> What should I do? Do you know how many

times I've run out of tampons? How many
times, with all my scattered and irresponsible
forgetfulness, that I've needed something and
someone has met my need? I have 50 people
right now who would bail me out like this!

Tania:
You obviously can't give her $100, but you
could pay to have tampons delivered to her.
Also, can I please have the names of all the
people who would give you $100 for tampons? I
need these people as my friends right now.

My life couldn't possibly be more different from Tommy's
mom's. After spending twenty years on the street, she has spent
the last eighteen months—since Tommy left my home and re-
joined her—in various rehabs and shelters and programs. She
has never had a job. She has no family and few actual friends.
She has no one to call, for example, when she needs tampons
and doesn't have a dollar to her name.

Like her, I've dropped the ball many times. I've forgotten to
pay a bill on time, missed a WIC appointment, failed to line
up a babysitter. But as a middle-class woman with a savings
account and a support system, none of these things have ever
brought anything more than minor inconvenience. When I forget to pay my bill, my overdraft protection covers my late fees.
When I miss my WIC appointment, I simply drop the seventeen
dollars for formula rather than getting it for free. When I fail
to line up a sitter, I call my husband and say, "I need you to
work from home."

My life is covered in great privilege that makes up for many
of the missteps and failings I've had as a mom. Our foster children's parents usually don't share in that privilege. A mistake
isn't easily repaired and can have devastating consequences. "It

takes a village," of course, and many of our kids' parents don't have a village. "Everyone needs a second chance," and most of our kids' parents have used up their chances.

The more aware I am of my own failings and my own need for help, the more prone I am to be willing to help or, at the very least, feel compassion for them in their need.

A Record of Wrongs

First Corinthians 13:5 refers to keeping a "record of wrongs" (NIV), which is basically the opposite of love. I've never put pen to paper with an actual record of wrongs, but I've certainly composed many. In my mind's eye, I can see the imaginary lists of wrongs of my kids' parents, usually starting before their child's birth and extending through today. It's very easy to inventory the wrongs of these parents—against themselves, their kids, me.

But doing everything in love[4] means ripping up the proverbial list of wrongs and switching the lens with which I see my kids' parents. And here's the punch line: the way I see my kids' parents actually has nothing to do with my kids' parents and everything to do with my own heart. I don't believe a false narrative or focus on some imaginary picture of who they are. I look away from them completely. I look to my God.

When I'm more aware of my own failings than I am of another's, when I'm more aware of the things I've been gifted than the things I'm giving, when I'm more aware of the love I've received than the love I offer, I can become a true lover of others. Even, and especially, my kids' parents.

eleven

But What about My Kids?

I sat in my car in the gas station parking lot. Through blurring tears, I texted my husband: "I don't want to do this anymore. It's one thing to go through this ourselves, but to do it to everyone else around us too. . . . We keep putting the kids through this, and it's not fair to them." We were saying goodbye to our fourth child in one year, and it was beginning to take an emotional toll on all of us. "I think we should quit," I typed.

The question I'm most often asked by parents considering foster care is "But what about my kids?" As parents, our first job and primary concern is always our kids. We wonder, *Will I be able to protect them from harm and heartbreak? Will I be able to give them enough attention and affection? Will I—in some way—end up sacrificing my child for someone else's?*

House Rules

I'm a bit of a rule breaker by nature. When DCPP asked us to write out a list of "house rules," I scoffed at the directive.

We scrawled a few words about not yelling or hitting or stealing, but the real "house rules" aren't for the family. They're for me and my husband. They're a list of principles held in our hearts that we cling to as we lead our family on this path—guidelines that help us do this foster care thing well as a family unit while still protecting and prioritizing our forever family.

1. We Are a Family on a Mission

Coasting isn't an option. Ease isn't on the menu. We are followers of Christ, which means we follow—into service, into action, into mission.

As foster parents, the way we "defend the fatherless" (Isaiah 1:17 NKJV) is by inviting them into our homes to become one of us. Part of that "us" includes our children, who are along for the ride of anything and everything the family takes on as a unit. They're the big sisters and the little brothers, the welcomers and the "Let me show you around"-ers, the babysitters and the buddies, the roommates and the mentors.

Sometimes our forever kids are uniquely equipped to help our foster children in ways that we can't. My friend Rachel once had a five-year-old foster son who was having recurring nightmares that woke him several times each night. The simple solution would have been to bring him into her bedroom where he would feel safe and she'd be able to quickly comfort him, but of course DCF wouldn't allow this. So she decided to put him in the bedroom of her five-year-old biological son, Jackson, for a period so he wouldn't be alone. After a little while, the nightmares subsided, and Rachel transitioned him back into his own room. One morning he woke up and said to her, "I woke up scared once last night, but then I thought of how Jackson sleeps in his bed all night. I knew if he could be brave, I could too." Rachel shared with me, "God used our five-year-old son to do what I couldn't."

Your children may embrace each foster placement as "sibling," or they may not. They may be very involved in providing care, befriending a peer, welcoming kids into the family, or they may not. But in one way or another, foster care will touch their lives significantly. It will serve them well to understand that together you are a family on a mission, ready to do the good works God has prepared for you,[1] deployed by you, the parent, in service to the Lord. We decide for ourselves and for our children: "As for me and my house, we will serve the LORD" (Joshua 24:15).

2. We Prepare Our Children

As parents, our job is to teach, talk, and train.[2] We teach our kids about God and about life, and when we're pulling them into mission with us, we teach them about the mission.

Our kids need to understand what foster care is all about. There are great resources and books that explain it, but the best resource will most certainly be *you*. Talk to your kids about why children are in foster care. Explain how sometimes parents have had hard lives and don't quite know how to create the right life for their kids, how some parents are sick in their body or brain and need to get healthy, how some parents don't have the things we have and need some extra help. Explain how every child deserves to be safe, and if they can't be safe in their homes, they sometimes have to leave their homes for a while. Explain that you'll be there for the kids for as long as their parents need help. Most of all, explain that sometimes it will be hard but that you are doing it because God loves these kids and parents, and He wants us to love them too.

Our children will experience sacrifices—time with parents, bedroom space, family busyness, the loss of siblings—but it will serve them well if we prepare them with as much information as we can, with as many tools as we're able. Our kids, as foster siblings, will have to access the same biblical truths that carry us, as foster parents, through this journey. Provide them with simple lessons from God's Word that they can begin to apply so that they will eventually say, "In him my heart trusts, and I am helped" (Psalm 28:7).

We have had so many conversations about foster care that my kids are able to regurgitate—and maybe even believe—the contradicting realities in a simple, childlike way. I remember when my four-year-old daughter, sitting with the baby in her arms, said, like a commercial for foster care but straight from deep down in her heart, "I wish we could adopt her, but she has a mommy. She's my sister now, but when her mommy's ready, she'll get to be with her again!" This is the fruit of intentionally *teaching* our kids a well-rounded, compassionate view of foster care.

3. We Ask and We Listen

We can easily become so consumed with a new little person and their needs and behaviors and caseworkers and court dates that we don't take the time to listen to our forever children. We assume they're fine, when they need us to ask them if they really are.

When my friend Jackie welcomed a teenage foster daughter, it disrupted the birth order of her three biological daughters. Her eleven-year-old daughter, Michaela, lost her role in the family as the oldest child as well her prized "own room." Relegated to middle child and stuck sharing a bedroom with her two little sisters, Michaela struggled with the transition. I believe the exact language was "I know I said I was willing to give up my room, but I want it back. She can sleep in a tent in the front yard for all I care."

My friend could have simply labeled her daughter an ungrateful brat, but she saw through the language and to the struggle that was driving it. Her daughter was questioning her place in the family, struggling to remember the why behind all the sacrifices she was making. Jackie began spending regular one-on-one time with Michaela. She invited her to share her heart and committed to really listening to her. She validated the parts of being a foster sibling that were especially difficult, reminded her of the excitement she first had in opening their home and giving up her room, reenvisioned her for the great gift their family was providing this girl, and thanked her for her sacrifices.

Prioritize one-on-one time with each child. Ask intentional questions about how they feel, what they're thinking, what they're experiencing. Guard yourself from a "Compared to these kids, your life is great; get over it" mentality, and really listen and hear. When our kids reveal their thoughts to us, they provide us with an invitation to speak into their hearts. We are able to show compassion and help them access and apply the gospel.

Especially with adopted children, we have to take the time to listen to everything they're feeling about foster care. Children being removed and placed, visits with biological family, or the loss of a sibling can all be triggering for our adopted children. Foster care often raises questions and emotions with one of my adopted children in particular. I make sure to take the time to flesh it out. I sit with her and look her in the eyes and ask, "Anything else?" and then "Anything else?" again. I want her to share her heart so that I can speak into her heart. I want her to ask questions so that I can answer them. And I always repeat over and over again, "Forever. Forever. Forever. You will never leave. You are our daughter forever."

4. We Consider Everyone's Opinions and Needs

I've heard some foster parents say, "If my children ever want to stop fostering, we would stop." I personally don't subscribe to that thinking, but I know many great parents who do. If your children ever communicate that they don't want a specific placement in the home or that they want to stop completely, I think it's helpful to question why. Is it the selfish resentment of sharing toys or a dark struggle with anxiety? Are they simply annoyed by a crying baby, or are they questioning their worth and place in the family? We need to be emotional detectives for our children. Foster care will bring challenges and sacrifices that will benefit our children, but it may sometimes bring trials that are too heavy for them to bear.

Maybe your kids aren't old enough or able to articulate their feelings or needs. Be aware of your kids' particular tendencies and struggles and personalities. For example, my son is a total alpha male, so I would never bring another boy his age into our home. It would be a disaster, and I don't need him to tell me that. I know him, and I know what he needs. Consider your children's needs and listen to their opinions.

5. We Share Honestly and with Boundaries

Babysitting my six nieces and nephews brought the kid count of my house to twelve for a few hours. Twelve kids under age ten, to be exact. Like our own family, my brother's kid break-down was two biological, two adopted, and two foster. The kids were playing in the living room while I washed the dishes. I was hearing, but I wasn't listening, until something caught my ear.

"Where's your dad, Mia?"

"He's in county," she answered innocently.

I wasn't going to shut down the conversation. There was nothing wrong with it, after all, and I certainly didn't want Mia to feel shame about the fact that her dad was, in fact, in the county jail. But I wasn't above distracting the group of them with sugar either.

"Hey, guys, who wants a cookie?"

"Yeah!" twelve little voices answered. The conversation was successfully shelved—temporarily.

As I put one of my kids to bed—the one who listens and wonders and holds in her heart—she asked, "Mommy? What is 'county'?" I knew what she was asking.

"Mia's dad is in jail," was my simple answer.

"Why is he in jail?" she wondered aloud.

I took a breath and dove in. "You remember when we talked about how Daniel's mom did drugs, and that's why she couldn't take care of him? Well, drugs are so dangerous that if you do them, sometimes you have to go to jail."

"If they're so dangerous," she pushed, "then why would someone do them?"

I mulled over my answer in my head before letting it out. "Some people have had hard lives, and they feel so scared and sad that they don't know what else to do to feel better. But I don't really know for sure. I've never met him, but I wouldn't be surprised if Mia's dad had a hard life. Should we pray for him, and for Mia?"

Our kids are exposed to a brokenness they wouldn't otherwise know if it weren't for foster care. They're well versed in addiction and family court in a way I never planned for them to be. While we try to be open and honest with *what* we share, we are careful about *how* we share. We talk about foster care like it's a privilege to play a part in fixing something broken. We speak of our foster children's parents with compassion and respect. We share about goodbyes like they're sad but not like they're bad. We explain that the parts that are hard are hard because they're important. We let our kids see our tears but not hear our fears.

While I don't want my kids to be too sheltered, it *is* my responsibility to shelter them—to protect them—from exposure to heartbreaking realities that are too heavy for their little hearts. I learned this from a story Nazi-Holocaust victim Corrie ten Boom shares of a time she asked her father a question he deemed too heavy:

> He turned to look at me, as he always did when answering a question, but to my surprise he said nothing. At last he stood up, lifted his traveling case from the rack above our heads and set it on the floor. "Will you carry it off the train, Corrie?" he said.
>
> I stood up and tugged at it. It was crammed with the watches and spare parts he had purchased that morning. "It's too heavy," I said.
>
> "Yes," he said, "and it would be a pretty poor father who would ask his little girl to carry such a load. It's the same way, Corrie, with knowledge. Some knowledge is too heavy for children. When you are older and stronger, you can bear it. For now you must trust me to carry it for you."[3]

Our forever kids are affected by the stories and timelines of the children we bring into our homes. They look to us to help them process, and they are trusting us to do it honestly. But we still carry much of the load, making sure not to burden them with a heaviness they cannot yet bear.

6. We Protect Our Family

If you ever want to be exposed to the good, the bad, and the ugly of humanity, just spend some time in an online "support" group. I launched a Facebook support group for foster parents, where more than twenty-five thousand parents request and provide encouragement and information, and it gets *real* weird. A few friends manage this group for me. Collectively, our least favorite interaction is when a foster child is hurting a biological child or putting the family at risk, and the foster parent asks for advice, only to be met with the snarky answer, "Well, what would you do if it was your biological child?"

Friends, for all my talk of "There's no difference" and "We love them just the same" and calling foster children "your children," I'm going to draw a line in the sand: You do not bear the same responsibility for your foster children that you do for your biological and adopted children. What a beautiful thing to step in for a child and love them like your own, but the reality is that they are *not* your own, not biologically, not legally, not before God. Maybe like one of the posters in my Facebook group, you have a situation where one of your foster children is putting your family at risk and you're not sure what you're supposed to do, how you should handle it. There's one thing that you never have to question: God has called you to protect and prioritize the children whom He has entrusted to you forever.[4]

The lesson of sacrificial love is one of the great gifts foster care provides to my children. I want my children to sacrifice, but I will never allow them to be the ones who are sacrificed.

The Benefits

You'll come across other "rules" too, maybe even some you'll learn the hard way. But as we weigh the risks and rewards of foster care for our forever children, the balances rise in the favor of *all* there is for our kids to gain. As my husband says, "One of the reasons we do foster care is *for* our children, so they'll learn about sacrificial love and service and following Jesus in hard ways." Foster care has been more than an opportunity for us to do good. It's done good for us.

Here are some of the benefits and lessons foster care has gifted our forever children:

It has put us on mission as a family. We all have a role to play, and we've enjoyed the unity and purpose of accomplishing kingdom work together. My daughter likes to tell people that I say I could never be a foster parent without her. And it's true; I do say that. My kids' service to our family and the kids we bring into the home is invaluable. Foster care teaches our kids what it looks like to be the hands and feet of Jesus.

We are able to expose our children to brokenness with a filter. I don't want my children to live in a bubble, but I don't want to just throw them to the wolves either. Foster care allows us to invite the brokenness of others into our home, where we can practice love and compassion in a safe environment. My children learn love and acceptance of others— maybe even those hard to love and accept. They learn what it means to be patient with others and come alongside them in their weakness.

We have grown in generosity and hospitality. Mother Teresa is credited with saying, "The problem with the world is that we draw the circle of our family too small." Welcoming children into our family has become a part of our family's DNA. Our definition of family—and what is "ours" in general—has become fluid, and my kids are learning that we are blessed to bless again. Our kids can be enthused about the idea of welcoming a sibling until the rubber hits the road of sharing toys and rooms and Mom. It is a blessing for our children to learn—sometimes the hard way—to live out generosity and hospitality.

We have discovered that the world is so much bigger. I'm grateful for the sacrifices my children have to make that teach them the world doesn't revolve around them. I pray that my kids' worlds are much bigger than their grades and soccer games, and my hope is that God uses foster care to expand their visions far past the hollow limitations of the "American dream."

We have learned empathy. We put a face and name to the need. Rather than praying for a theoretical group of people who are out there somewhere, my kids have learned what it looks like to love and pray for and walk with people in addiction and poverty and need. They've learned the backstory and struggle of people they maybe would have otherwise villainized, and they're learning what it looks like to approach those people with humility.

We have learned lessons on loss and grief. Our children *will* experience loss and grief in their lives. As parents, we want to protect our children from all sadness, when maybe the more loving and helpful thing would be to teach them how to grieve well. We have the opportunity to model healthy grieving to our kids and teach them what it looks like to walk through hard things.

We have learned gratitude. Our children are among the wealthiest and most privileged children ever to live on planet Earth. Chances are that yours, like mine, struggle with entitlement and ingratitude. Understanding the experiences of those who have less—materially and otherwise—helps to build gratitude.

We have found that love is costly. As our kids learn to sacrifice, to love those who can be hard to love, and to walk through loss, they begin to understand that love is costly. This is a helpful lesson for life and relationships, but more than that, it points them to the love that Jesus has for them. As they learn to love sacrificially, they grow in their understanding of the sacrificial love they have been shown through the gospel.

I sat with a group of foster friends and asked them about some of the benefits foster care has provided their children. Their answers helped form the list above. Finally, one of my friends looked at me with tears and said, "There have been so many times that I've stepped back and thought, *There's nothing I could have done to teach this.*"

Many of the lessons of foster care can't be contrived or created. They have to be walked through; they can only be earned. Foster care will certainly bring trials and sorrows to our children, but it will always provide them with great lessons about life and love, God and people. And those are invaluable lessons, priceless gifts.

The Other Risk

The decision to become a foster parent, the decision to say yes to each child since, has always been weighed with the best interests of our forever children. Our responsibility to them is primary. Protecting and prioritizing them must come first.

But along with considering the risks of bringing foster children into our home, we've considered the risks of not doing so. I want to protect my children from heartbreak and from danger and from difficulty. But really I want to protect them from so much more. I want to protect them from going through life thinking the world is about them, from the lie that following Jesus is always easy or that God is some magic genie who exists to serve our wishes, from the illusion that everyone lives the same charmed lives that they do. I want to protect them from a selfish, wasted life.

My dreams for my kids are bigger and better than health and wealth and happiness. I dream that my kids will love and live for Jesus above all, that they'll follow wherever He calls. I dream that they will live radically and love selflessly and serve sacrificially. I know that my dreaming and my training can't do this in their hearts—only God can do that—but I think that this foster sibling life is good training ground for these dreams.

twelve

I Don't Want to Hand
Her Over Today

can name my very lowest of foster parenting days: June 23, 2016. I've had sadder days, more confusing days, days with more stress, for sure. But this day was the lowest of low for me. It was the day that I first felt completely powerless to protect one of my children. The day with the really hard visit.

I spent the morning packing for a day at the shore. We were making the hour drive for a family reunion of sorts, a day at the beach with extended family we saw twice a year. With a seven-year-old, four-year-old, two-year-old, and one-year-old, it took me approximately three hours to pack and prepare. The plan was to get them in the car and feed them as soon as we arrived. I was in my typical getting-ready-for-the-shore mode, which is me at my momming best: yelling and sweating, stuffing gear in the trunk, and driving back home seven times because I forgot something.

Halfway to the beach, I got a call from my foster daughter's worker: "The final visit with Dad was just scheduled. It's in an hour and a half."

"That's not going to work for us," I responded. "We're on our way to the shore."

"It has to work. It's going to work. I'll send someone to the beach to pick her up."

This is the appointment we had been waiting for—a court-ordered visit with a lawyer and a doctor and a very dangerous dad. "She hasn't seen him in a year, she's terrified of him, she'll scream the whole time," I moaned to the worker when she told me it needed to happen.

"That's the hope!" was the worker's transparent and tragic response. I thought of the doctors' oath to "do no harm," and I wished social workers had to make the same pledge. My little girl was the chess piece in this game for her custody. She was being ripped out of my hands and placed on the board to play her part. Show up and scream. Prove to everyone just how very scared you are of this very scary man.

A short while later, I dragged my family onto the beach, stomped back out to the boardwalk, and buckled my girl into an unknown worker's car with a kiss. They pulled away, and I realized, *I forgot to send her lunch.* That was it. That was enough to put this Italian foodie mama bear over the edge from temper tantrum to rage pool. *Sitting in the car for an hour . . . missing the family beach day . . . about to sit for another hour . . . an appointment for which your part is to act traumatized because, oh yeah, you're actually being traumatized . . . all without lunch.*

I hate foster care. I hate the stupid judges with their stupid orders. I hate the parents, and I hate what they've done to these kids. I hate the workers and what they continue to do to them. I hate the disgusting part I play in this disgusting game of this joke of a system. I hate, hate, hate these stupid visits. I hate this feeling. I hate this life. I hate it.

My stomach aches now just remembering it. After three years of foster parenting, I had finally hit a wall. I felt completely powerless to do what I thought was best for this child. I *was* completely powerless to do what was best for this child. I was actively handing over my child to be harmed for this harmlessly titled outing named a "visit." She would be hungry and tired and confused and terrified and traumatized, and here I was playing my little part and following the rules and buckling her in for the ride.

You Signed Up for This

Visits with biological parents are one of the hard parts of this hard life. Sometimes parents are wonderful and kids are thrilled to go and perfectly content once they return—the picture of family-reunifying happiness. Many times the visits mirror more what my brother texted me this morning: "Handing Jeremiah over for visits is absolutely gut-wrenching. I feel physically sick. Foster care sucks. *That* should be on one of your T-shirts."

Foster parent, I'm about to tell you the least helpful thing any person can ever tell any other person in any situation: You signed up for this. As a foster parent, letting your child go for visits (as if you had a choice) and helping these times to be successful are a huge part of what you signed up for.

Visits are one of the most important parts of the reunification process and are therefore one of the most important parts of foster care. Visits are the opportunity for a parent and child to maintain (or form) a bond. They're the reminder to a fighting parent: *This is what you're fighting for.* They're the opportunity for workers to observe and teach. They're the space for a child—even a child who is angry or afraid or confused—to spend time with their parent. There have been many times I've hated my kids' visits with their parents, times I've felt like the visits were harmful to them. But I also believe visits are important times for my kids and their parents to share together.

In fact, as a parent who has adopted from foster care, I see how my kids' visits with biological parents ended up being important for both my children's cases and my children's identities. The seemingly—and maybe even actually—traumatizing visits ended up being a vital part of what built the case for the necessity of adoption. More than that, though, for one of my children, visits provided the only memories and moments they have of their parents. Even though, at the time, they were very difficult, we are able to recount memories together and talk about their visit times with fondness and appreciation.

You Have to Be a Sociopath

I sat across from a child psychologist who works in the foster care field, a little old lady with a generous smile and huge reputation. "You have to be a sociopath," she confided, "to do what they ask you to do. To love a child, completely and as your own, but be willing to hand them over in an instant, you have to be a sociopath. Only a sociopath can do that."

Parents, we weren't wired with a willingness to hand over our children. It goes against our very God-given nature as parents. Our instincts are to protect and preserve. Those instincts are divinely wired into our brains and bodies, and they're not easy to override. But "He who call[ed] you is faithful" (1 Thessalonians 5:24), and you can expect a high measure of grace to meet the high order.

Handing my kids over for visits used to be extremely difficult, but it has gotten much easier. I'm 90 percent sure it's not because I've become a sociopath. But I have gotten much better at disconnecting myself from the pathos of it—the suffering, the experience, the emotion. I have essentially learned to flick off the "mom switch" for a moment. How? (You're really starting to think I'm a sociopath now, aren't you?) I remember this one small and perspective-shaping belief that trumps and shatters every instinct and emotion I face: Even when I can't be with my children as their mother, they are always in the care of their Father. *They are always in the care of their Father.* He hems them in, behind and before, laying His hand on them.[1] They couldn't escape His presence if they tried. Wherever they go, He is there.[2]

It's a strange thing to put off and put on the role of mother or father, but it's sort of inherent to the "job," isn't it? One moment a child I've never met exists in the world without me; the next moment they show up at my door and not only am I responsible for them, I am—functionally—mom to them. Visits are a microcosm of that reality, a putting on and off of the cloak of parenthood. The great truth that protects me from the whiplash of emotions is remembering whom these children actually belong to, whose protection they've always been under. These children are God's: loved by Him, under His care, within His loving plan. It is He who made them, and they are His.[3] Being a foster parent means entrusting them to Him for their time before my home, once they've left my home, and for these visits outside of my home.

You know your kid has been through a lot when she calls her social worker her best friend. That's exactly what mine did. Ms. Laurie was my foster daughter's "best friend." Ask her about her visits, and she'd barely mention the mother who was most certainly there, but on and on she'd go about Ms. Laurie and all they did together.

The day came when this little girl had to visit her dad, for the first time in a year, in jail. If you're picturing full orange jumpsuit, handcuffs, ankle cuffs—the works—you're right. I was terrified; she was terrified. But Ms. Laurie would be there. As Laurie picked her up to bring her to this visit, I looked her in the eyes and thanked her as heartily as I've ever thanked anyone before: "The fact that you're going to be with her is the only reason I'm okay, the only reason she'll be okay. It means everything. Thank you."

Putting my child in someone else's arms for such a terrifying moment was painful, but *whose* arms I was placing her in made all the difference. That's what this foster care life is. It's a constant placing of your child in someone else's hands—literally and actually, in workers' and judges' and lawyers' hands. And it's a placing of your child, figuratively and spiritually—but also, in a very real way, *actually*—in God's hands.

We have to make this connection and remind ourselves of just who this God is we're entrusting our children to. We hand our children over to a God who never changes, who tells us about Himself, who we can trust to be who He says He is.

- He is always with them.
  - "The LORD your God is with you wherever you go." (Joshua 1:9)
  - "My presence will go with you." (Exodus 33:14)
  The God of the universe accompanies your children every time they leave your sight. Want to talk supervised visits? Yeah, God Almighty is there supervising. We'd all choose to be there to help and comfort and control if we could. But with Him there, who needs you?

- He is for them.
  - "The LORD is on my side; I will not fear. What can man do to me?" (Psalm 118:6)

    There's no greater father figure, mama bear, parent protector. God is for our kids. They are in good hands. What can any person do?
- He can help them.
  - "God is our refuge and strength, an ever-present help in trouble." (Psalm 46:1 NIV)

    When we cannot be present, God is ever present. When we want to be able to give our children all things, He is actually able to give everything: safety and strength and peace. Our presence is limited even when we are present. He is able to provide all that our kids need.
- He can comfort them.
  - "I will fear no evil, for you are with me; your rod and your staff, they comfort me." (Psalm 23:4)
  - "May your unfailing love be my comfort." (Psalm 119:76 NIV)

    Our abilities as parents are constricted by the limitations of proximity and language and other human constraints. God is able to supernaturally and automatically provide comfort to our children that we can't even comprehend. He can touch their souls and meet their hearts and bring consolation to their unspoken needs.
- He has a good plan for them.
  - "The LORD is good to all, and His tender mercies are over all His works." (Psalm 145:9 NKJV)

    God is accomplishing something for our children that He has ordained in His always-sovereign, only-good plan. If they are His children, His plans will ultimately be for their good—the hard, the sad, all of it. God is accomplishing something that we can trust, that we will eventually—even if only in heaven—celebrate.

These aren't just verses for us as adults. These truths are for our children. We can believe these truths for them. We can remind our children of these truths. We can trust that these truths apply to them, even if our children may not understand them. The character of God can provide comfort to us and to our children.

You Can Do Hard Things

How could I even choose the stories to share in this chapter? Yeah, there's the June 23, 2016, story. And there's the orange jumpsuit and handcuff story. But there's also the four-hour drive back and forth to rehab story. The social worker gets in a car accident on the way to the visit story. The visits with just-high-enough-to-get-away-with-it parent and dangerous criminal and sex offender stories. Not to mention, the parents falling asleep and sitting on their phones, ignoring their kids *non*stories. I've had countless times—*countless*—of having to do the truly hard task of releasing my child to a situation I would never, ever, not ever choose for them.

My friend Lisa compares it to breastfeeding. Ladies, if you nursed any of your kids, you know what she's talking about. Guys, just trust me. You know it's going to hurt, you know it will feel awful, but you suck it up and you let out a primal scream, and you do it.

You are a parent. Not only a parent, a *foster* parent. You can do hard things. But not in some cliché "I'm a foster parent—what's your superpower?" sort of way. In a weak and dependent and truly needy sort of way. I can do all things—even when I "can't"—through Christ who gives me the strength.[4] You can do hard things, not because "you've got this" but because you are carried by the One who does.

A Love-Hate Relationship

If you don't equally love and hate visits, are you even a foster parent?

I hate them. I hate the sugar and the smoke-covered clothes and the too-late bedtimes. I hate the lack of control, the no-shows, the sadness before and after, the way it disrupts our family. And I love them. I love that my kids get to be with their parents, that their parents get face-to-face reminders of the precious ones they're fighting for. I love that the sacred bond between them gets a fighting chance, that these times will be meaningful to my kids no matter where they spend their forever.

I often feel the hate, but I choose the love. Yes, because this whole thing is about so much more than my feelings. But also because the realities written above—the truths of God that I've so often had to remember and believe—trump and transform my feelings.

Your God—*your child's God*—is good. He is with them. He is for them. He can help them and comfort them, and He has a good plan for them. And so, as reluctantly as you may place your child in someone else's hands, you can wholeheartedly leave them where in reality they've been all along. In God's hands.

thirteen

Self-Care Isn't Selfish

It was like a sitcom where one character laughs and laughs uncontrollably and the other character looks on confused, not getting that *they* are the butt of the joke.

My best friend Julie asked about a foster care conference I was speaking at. "What's the topic of your breakout?" she asked.

"Self-care," I answered matter-of-factly, like there was nothing at all unusual about it.

"Self-care?"—awkward silence, incredulous stare—"*Self-care?!*"—hysterical laughter, more hysterical laughter—"Self-care"—regaining her breath, enjoying her own joke.

I was the butt of the joke, to be clear.

My friend laughed for good reason. Honestly, I want to laugh at myself now, thinking about it. It was only a year ago, but looking back, I realize that I had absolutely no idea what *self-care* meant. In fact, I was infamously bad at self-care. In fact, if someone said, "Name the person you know who is the worst at taking care of herself," most people in my life would have named me. For years I've worked too hard and taken on too many responsibilities and cared for too many kids while subsisting on chocolate for breakfast, coffee all day, and inordinate amounts of pasta. I don't exercise, I have no hobbies, I average five hours of sleep a day, and I'm constantly stressed. I'm getting better, I am. But honestly, I'm still learning.

Self-care is all the rage these days, but I'm guessing that many view it as incorrectly as I did a year ago. Our culture can view self-care as massages and midday lattes, falling somewhere between self-indulgence and self-worship. The church can view self-care as self-glorifying and self-centered, pursuing enjoyment and comfort for the sake of itself. Parents can view self-care as frivolous and optional, something they have no time for and always the first thing on the list to go. But self-care isn't any of these things.

True self-care is not indulgent. It's not about adding anything into your life. It's not about extravagant, expensive experiences or long periods alone. It's not about doing anything, really. True self-care is a perspective shift that is simply and purely about taking care of yourself. It's motivated by love, driven by wisdom, and walked out in humility.

Secondary Trauma

I hope you've learned about secondary trauma, but I wouldn't be surprised if you haven't. Every foster parent is at risk for it, and many don't even know it exists. As a foster parent, you have people who have experienced trauma—to one extent or another—living in your home. The thing about trauma is that it doesn't stay bundled up in the confines of one person's experience. It bleeds out over everyone around it too. Secondary trauma is the residual effect of loving someone who has been through the things our kids have been through. Basically, secondary trauma is the trauma we incur from caring for the traumatized.

Like those of its mother, post-traumatic stress disorder, the symptoms of secondary trauma are pervasive: sadness, anxiety, decreased concentration, changes in sleep and appetite, and heightened startle response, just to name a few.[1] If you haven't experienced this, it may all seem a bit dramatic and overblown. If you have experienced this, maybe you're seeing yourself in this list and cartoon lightbulbs are appearing over your head. Last year, I had my own lightbulb moment. My body had become weak, my emotions were unmanageable, my mind wasn't clear. I was experiencing that list of symptoms above. My mom, in typical mom fashion, gave me a stern talking to: "You need to act like you're recovering from strep throat [since, side note, I had strep throat five times last year because my body is smarter than my brain and knew I needed to slow down before the rest of me did]. Follow the same recovery list: drink water and take naps and eat vegetables and *take care of yourself*."

Self-care can be preventative or it can be prescriptive. We need it, but we often don't realize we need it—or buy into the fact that we need it—until it's too late. As a foster parent, you are at serious risk for incurring secondary trauma, so take it from me: Do yourself a favor and let your self-care be preventative.[2]

Sometimes clichés are clichés for a reason, right? Like the "Put on your own oxygen mask before putting on your child's mask if the plane is going down" rule. This is the perfect picture of self-care. This idea of helping yourself before you can help someone else is counterintuitive to parenthood. So much so that despite the dozens of times I've heard a flight attendant give this speech, I'm 90 percent sure if I was in an airplane with my children and the masks popped out, I would put on each of their masks before my own. I *know* better! I *know* that I'm supposed to put on my own first. I *know* this scenario leaves me passed out, helpless, and worthless to my children. But it's so anti-instinctual to take care of myself first that, even though I know better, I'm not sure I would do it. Me, personally? I have to be convinced that this idea of self-care is about *them* and for *their* good and not just about me being a happier version of myself.

I said before that true self-care is motivated by love, driven by wisdom, and walked out in humility. Let's look at each of these.

Motivated by Love

"*Be devoted to one another in love*" *(Romans 12:10 NIV).* My devotion to my children makes me want to be the best mom I can possibly be. It's very hard for me to walk in love, show love, or teach love when I'm, for example, chronically stressed or completely exhausted. My love for my kids motivates my commitment to practice self-care, even when it feels like it's not important or I don't have time. It *has* to be important. I *have* to make time. Scripture "urges" me to love my children,[3] and it is my love for them that persuades me to pursue whatever will help me love them better.

Driven by Wisdom

"*Be very careful, then, how you live—not as unwise but as wise, making the most of every opportunity*" *(Ephesians 5:15–16 NIV).* Our life and being are gifts from God, and He has called us to be good stewards of them.[4] God created our bodies and souls with certain needs. Needing sunlight and water, food and rest, community and laughter, our bodies are not self-sustaining. We were designed to *need*, to adopt rhythms of input and output that are part of the created order. To think that we are somehow above the needs that God placed within our bodies and brains and selves is utter foolishness. I confess that I have lived foolishly and in disobedience, expecting to be able to ignore my own needs yet still be able to abundantly meet the needs of others.

Walked Out in Humility

"On the seventh day God finished his work that he had done, and he rested on the seventh day from all his work that he had done" (Genesis 2:2). Does this section need any more than the reminder that God Himself rested? And He was not limited by the constraints of a human body and fallen world! We can gather from this verse that rest is in and of itself a holy and worthy pursuit. Rest—and all that word embodies of physical rest, emotional rest, mental rest, spiritual rest—is not simply about recharging a limited body. It is about pursuing a divine discipline.

This means dismantling the savior complex so many of us lean toward. "The God who made the world and everything in it . . . is not served by human hands, as if he needed anything" (Acts 17:24–25 NIV). God is not dependent on us to accomplish anything. We can throw off the burden of being everything to everyone. That is not a weight we have to carry. It is not a weight we have the grace to carry because it is not a weight God has called us to. We can simply accept and remember (and be grateful for) the fact that we are not God.

What Would Jesus Do?

If you're still not convinced, let's look more at how the Lord Himself held this idea of self-care.

"Jesus often withdrew to lonely places and prayed" (Luke 5:16 NIV). He left the crowds with all their needs behind to be with His friends and to take a nap.[5] He "dismissed the crowds . . . [and] went up on the mountain by himself to pray" (Matthew 14:23). When He heard about His cousin John being killed, "He withdrew by boat privately to a solitary place" (Matthew 14:13 NIV), and on another occasion, "He entered a house and did not want anyone to know it" (Mark 7:24 NIV). (Anyone else feeling better about hiding in the closet from your kids?)

Many times we read of Jesus walking beside the Sea of Galilee or the lake, hiking on mountainsides or along grain fields, and spending time with His friends and His Father.[6] Jesus lived with single-minded vision to "do the will of him who sent [him]" (John 6:38 NIV), yet we see a lifestyle of rest and fellowship and communion with the Father. He lived on mission in a way that no human ever has or ever will, yet He regularly rested. Of course, Jesus is God. He could have simply downloaded a divine dose of strength and power in a moment, yet He modeled for us a picture of intentionally recharged mission.

And what about Jesus's expectations of His followers? When His disciples were run ragged "because so many people were coming and going that they did not even have a chance to eat, he said to them, 'Come with me by yourselves to a quiet place and get some rest'" (Mark 6:31 NIV). Rather than sending the five thousand away to get their own food, He "directed the people to sit down on the grass," and He gave them fish and bread, and "they all ate and were satisfied" (Matthew 14:19–20 NIV).

And then there's our friend Martha. (Any Marthas in the house? Raise a stressed, exhausted, "Who's going to do it if I don't?" hand with me if that's you.) When she was "distracted with much serving" (Luke 10:40) and "anxious and troubled about many things" (v. 41), Jesus called her to the most important task, the "good portion, which will not be taken" (v. 42) of simply sitting at His feet. Jesus loved the people around Him and provided them with healing and food and rest and comfort. We are His beloved, and His heart is the same for us as it was for them.

Are you convinced? Or are you (as I would be) tempted to skip ahead to the "important" parts of the book about becoming a better foster parent? Friend, stop. Reread the Scriptures above. Hear God's heart for you. See the example He laid out for you. Embrace humility and believe Him. Once you're convinced—really, actually convinced—consider what self-care may actually look like in your life. No one can tell you how to "do" self-care. It's not a checklist or to-do list. It's a perspective shift. But for the sake of clarity and application, here's a view into what it's looked like in my life.

Enjoy Life

"A merry heart doeth good like a medicine" (*Proverbs 17:22 KJV*). Let's start with the most basic and commonly understood application of self-care. God created you with an innate ability to experience joy and pleasure. Taste buds and oxytocin and sexual organs and eyes that see color all point to His design for us to experience enjoyment. When we find our ultimate joy in Him and experience all His good gifts as gifts, we worship Him through our enjoyment of them.[7] He's a good Father who loves to bring joy to His children. What do you enjoy? I love the Beatles and Mexican food and writing, local IPAs and coffee, and watching Netflix and chilling with my husband. Maybe you love crocheting or hunting or writing poetry or playing basketball. I sat in a self-care breakout once where a woman said she enjoyed her bug collection—so, you know, to each their own. Whatever you enjoy, take the time to enjoy it.

Make the time to pursue the good medicine of a merry heart and worship your Father who is the Giver of "every good and perfect gift" (James 1:17 NIV).

Be Healthy

"Do you not know that your body is a temple of the Holy Spirit within you, whom you have from God? You are not your own, for you were bought with a price. So glorify God in your body" (1 Corinthians 6:19–20). Entire books are written on theories and methods for pursuing health, and I am the last person on earth who would write one. But you know all the things: sleep, eat healthy foods, drink water, be outside, exercise. Start with one practice and call it what it is: a spiritual discipline of humility and an act of self-care and love. I've begun walking thirty minutes a day and eating healthier foods for body health, and meditating for ten minutes a day for brain health. I don't enjoy these things, but I practice them in faith and obedience.

I would be remiss if I didn't address mental health. Practicing self-care can be a safeguard for mental health, but it's not a cure for mental illness. If you had diabetes or cancer, you would go to the doctor and take medicine; you would spend whatever time and money it took to pursue health. But for some reason, we're more prone to a "pull yourself up by your own bootstraps" approach to mental health. About a year ago, I realized I needed professional help. I was living in a state of chronic stress and anxiety, and my mental health was deteriorating. I was experiencing burnout and the symptoms of secondary trauma. I began seeing a therapist and intentionally building self-care into my life. Around the same time, my best friend and one of the godliest women I know found herself in a similar place and began taking an antidepressant that made all the difference for her. We're two average, Jesus-loving, "not crazy" women who've experienced the grace of God through professional mental health care.

Slow Down and Be Intentional

"Devote yourselves to prayer, being watchful and thankful" *(Colossians 4:2 NIV)*. The stress level in my home multiplies when I parent in a way that's reactionary and off the cuff. Too often this is the only kind of parenting I'm capable of because I'm not slowing down enough to be prayerful and intentional. For me, waking before my kids has made all the difference. It may seem crazy to include "Wake up at 5:30 a.m." as a strategy for self-care, but when I was able to slow down enough to consider my children's needs and intentionally care for them, the chaos in my home began to decrease.

I prayerfully consider the times in our day that are challenging, what worked the day before and what didn't, how each child is specifically struggling and could use encouragement and training. I proactively reorient and reconsider how I can better serve my children. I start off the day ready to meet them with love and intentionality rather than playing catch-up to whatever may come.

Be Grateful

"Give thanks to the LORD, for he is good, for his steadfast love endures forever" *(Psalm 136:1)*. I naturally struggle with discontentment and ingratitude. I always want life to be an adventure, and I can feel dissatisfied with average, "normal" life. This is an area where I've seen the Lord truly transform my heart and perspective. God has helped me understand that as someone who deserves nothing and yet has so much, I have received every single thing as a gift directly from His hand. The discipline of practicing gratitude has brought more joy and

peace to my life than any single practice. I've learned to find great joy in the small things—a warm shower, an encouraging text from a friend, a beautiful sunset—and I've learned to live in awe and worship for the huge things—a loving husband, a safe country, salvation itself.

I'm also learning to transform the hard things into gratitude. Framed on my wall are the words "There is always, always, always something to be grateful for." I find the most helpful practice of gratitude to be searching for that thing—the thing to be grateful for—in the most difficult of circumstances. When a challenging court order comes, a worker drops the ball, a child's behavior takes a turn for the worse, I search. I look at the difficulty, and I turn it in my heart again and again until I'm able to point to something. I write it down, I start a list, and then I go back and search for a second, a third thing to be grateful for. I keep searching until my heart has reoriented to a place of gratitude, of seeing grace in the midst of the challenging.

Gratitude sees that everything comes from the hand of God, and so everything is ultimately a gift from Him.[8] If He is sovereign and He is good, then everything I face is something to—in one way or another—be grateful for. It will all be used for my good, so it can all provoke thanks and praise.[9]

Live in Community

"Let us consider how we may spur one another on toward love and good deeds, not giving up meeting together" (*Hebrews 10:24–25 NIV*). Introverts, extroverts, every single number on the Enneagram, and every Myers-Briggs type: You were created to need others. I address living in community more in a later chapter, so I won't belabor my point here, but part of taking care of yourself includes allowing others to take care of you.

My four best friends provide my relational dose of self-care. Julie has been my BFF since we were thirteen years old, knows me better than anyone outside of my family, and might be my greatest encourager and harshest critic. If you want to hear a list of my very best and very worst qualities, she'd be happy to oblige. Amy is my soul mate and partner in crime. For twenty-plus years we've pursued the same interests and passions, but warning: you don't want to get between us if we disagree on something. Jayme is my sister-in-law of thirteen years and the person I do life with most in the world. She married my brother (who is pretty much the male version of me), so she knows how to put up with me and understands all the inner workings of our family. Hannah is my sister-in-law (she married the other brother) and business partner—we share the friend-family-work trifecta of connection. She loves my kids better and deeper than almost anyone else and would, for sure, give me the shirt off her back. Together the five of us have nineteen kids through birth, adoption, and foster care. When we get together, we talk about *everything*, eat underbaked brownies, and make fun of each other. We also pour out our hearts, call each other out, and cheer each other on. Letting them care for me—and caring for them—is one of the things that is most rejuvenating to me. Spending time with these four is top of my list of self-care.

We were created to need other people, and we won't thrive unless we are living life with them. You are in need of the encouragement and example and service *of* others, and you will also experience the great joy of being an encouragement and example and servant *to* others.

Return to the Source

"My soul finds rest in God" *(Psalm 62:1 NIV)*. This isn't another option on a list of ways to practice self-care. This is

the answer for the only true source of rest, peace, and joy. This is the foundation of an abundant life. I'm not talking about checking "devotions" off your to-do list or taking a magic pill to start off your day right. I'm talking about communing with the almighty God. The truest form of self-care means beginning at the beginning: acknowledging that we were created to know and worship God and embracing that wholeness is found in being "filled with all the fullness of God" (Ephesians 3:19) through knowing the love of Christ.

The Bible isn't just a book, and it's not just a collection of words about God. It's the way we actually spend time with and come to know the living God.

Do everything you can to create or protect time to commune with God. Keep your phone plugged in on a separate floor, go to bed earlier and wake earlier, hide in your closet during nap time or in your car before work. Treat it like it's life and death, because it is *life*. Talk to God randomly throughout the day and specifically in intentionally set-aside times. Hear from Him through His Word—you'll find Jesus in the book of John, encouragement in Isaiah or Philippians, worship in the Psalms. Learn from other saints through books and devotionals that point you to Scripture. Sing to your soul and your God as you listen to music that proclaims truth. Gather with God's people. Meditate. Fast. Practice the disciplines and the gifts He has provided to reveal Himself to you.

The quest for peace and rest will always end fruitlessly if we search outside of Him. As Augustine wrote, "Because you have made us for yourself, our hearts are restless till they find their rest in thee."[10]

Jesus calls to you in your weariness to find in Him all that you need: "Come to me, all who labor and are heavy laden, and I will give you rest. Take my yoke upon you, and learn from me, for I am gentle and lowly in heart, and you will find rest for your souls. For my yoke is easy, and my burden is light" (Matthew 11:28–30).

You Don't Have Time Not To

I have a penchant for running out of gas. I'm not talking metaphorically here. I mean my actual gas tank actually running out of gas. I don't *want* to run out of gas. It's just that sometimes it feels more pressing to do one more thing and get to one more place. *I need this and the kids need that and we have to get there and I'll take care of it later.* Then I'm left empty and stranded and no good to anyone. In the moment, *I don't have time for this* feels logical. But the reality is, I don't have the time *not* to.

My children deserve more *from* me, certainly. But also, my Father *has* more *for* me. The idea of self-care isn't a call for me to find ways to fill myself with more energy, more pleasure, *more, more, more.* It's an invitation to be filled by the Source, to find rest in His presence, to find strength in His Spirit. It's an invitation to find the abundant life He offers through submitting to the limitations and needs He has placed within my body and on my days.

"*He* restores my soul" (Psalm 23:3, emphasis mine). When I am motivated by love—by my love for my children, but more importantly, by His love for me—I'm freed from the frantic pursuit of trying to be enough in and of myself. I am not enough; my status quo is empty. I must remain close to the Source to be filled and to find the strength to care for myself so I can care for those He has entrusted to me.

fourteen

Social Workers and Therapists and Lawyers—Oh My!

T hey lie; they always lie. But God is a revealer of truth." My friend Sandy oozes love and joy and humility. She sees the best in people, and she wasn't being cynical when she stated matter-of-factly the reality she faced over and over again: *They always lie.*

Sandy's story is like that of so many other foster parents. Three kids placed without a mention of known abuse—the kind of abuse that too often leads to the abused becoming the abuser, the kind of abuse a foster parent *needs* to know about. And yet not a word. Then "Yes, I told you that," and "Well, it was never really confirmed anyway." Bullying and threatening, denying and blame-shifting. A worker saying anything and everything she can just to get kids in "beds" so she can be on her way home for the night. And Sandy's family left standing in the wreckage of it all. With their own children to consider and protect, they were left to sort through the web of lies to find the truth, to answer, "What now?"

I've heard it said that foster care is the ultimate form of hospitality. The call to invite someone to feel welcomed by your family is fully realized in inviting them to be welcomed and to actually *become* family. Foster care is a lived-out picture of the command to "show hospitality" (1 Peter 4:9).

Little did I know before becoming a foster parent that accompanying every child through my door would be a parade of social workers, nurses, therapists, lawyers, advocates, supervisors, transporters, and others whom I'll affectionately address as "workers" from this point forward. All of a sudden, a slew of people come into your home, invade your life, and sometimes seem to have more control over your life than you do.

Things have calmed down in the Finn household since the times when we had three foster children with open cases and a different entourage trailing behind each. I clearly remember a time when I counted up my kids' weekly appointments to the whopping number of twelve. I shared the number with every person my darkly circled eyes met, like a badge of honor for my busy week. The next week came, and I counted up the seven days' worth of appointments and hit that same number—twelve—again. And reality hit me with a flood of panic: this is our new norm.

When we become foster parents, a group of strangers become regular companions to our lives. People we probably wouldn't have chosen to be involved in our lives end up directing the course of them. We can't talk about surviving the trials of foster care without acknowledging the always-oh-so-delightful experience of dealing with social workers and therapists and lawyers (oh my!).

A How-To for Dealing with Workers

I hope you've had workers you love. I already spoke of my foster daughter's "best friend," Ms. Laurie. Goodness, I was so grateful for her. Then there was Doreen, one of the strongest advocates I've ever come across. Sally taught me everything about my kids' sensory needs. Jenn stood up in court and fought for my daughter not to be moved. Steve went above and beyond in supporting my foster child's mom. Jessenia called me immediately each time my foster son was removed again. Allyson was like a mama to my girl on her visits. Lianna single-handedly flipped the trajectory of my little boy's case. We've had many workers who have worked so hard and done their jobs so well.

I hate to list all these good things and then start the next sentence with a "but." *But* we've also had many workers who haven't worked hard or done their jobs well. You may have noticed I used someone else's names-were-changed story to open this chapter. I had a good reason for doing that. My home is still licensed and open, and if you're a foster parent who has experienced revenge and blacklisting from workers, you'll understand why I'm not sharing my list of names and attached offenses. I promise you, it would be ten times as long as the happy list above.

If you've been a foster parent for more than a day—scratch that—if you've even started the licensing process, I'm sure you've experienced a certain level of disappointment and inconvenience in relation to your workers.

Maybe you've suffered the devastation of lies and betrayals and threats. You've probably encountered dishonest workers, lazy individuals, incompetent players. At the very least, you've been touched by the inconveniences and lack of privacy and miscommunications of having all these people in your life. No foster parent gets through unscathed.

How do you deal with the difficulties these workers bring into your life? I have one very simple and completely world-changing perspective I want to propose: Workers are people, God's workmanship,[1] each a beloved life with a heart, a soul, a past, a future, an eternal destiny.

With the realization that workers are people, we have a blueprint for how God has called us to consider them and treat them. His Word speaks regularly about our interactions with others, particularly when we've been wronged.

Put on then, as God's chosen ones, holy and beloved, *compassionate hearts, kindness, humility, meekness, and patience, bearing with one another* and, if one has a complaint against another, *forgiving each other*; as the Lord has forgiven you, so you also must forgive. And above all these *put on love*, which binds everything together in perfect harmony. And let the peace of Christ rule in your hearts, to which indeed you were called in one body. And *be thankful.* (Colossians 3:12–15, emphasis mine)

Kindness and Compassion

"Put on . . . compassionate hearts, kindness, humility, meekness, and patience, bearing with one another" (Colossians 3:12–13). I can forget that workers are people. I can be tempted to see them simply as cogs in a system that appears to be, too often, pivoted against me and failing my foster child. But when I see them as precious souls, I am compelled to "walk in a manner worthy of the calling to which [I] have been called, with all humility and gentleness, with patience, bearing with [others] in love" (Ephesians 4:1–2).

My best friend Amy gently chides me to "judge charitably" whenever I'm ranting about one thing or another. Judging charitably means offering the generosity of the benefit of the doubt. It's starting with the assumption that most people are well intentioned and doing their best and facing the same roadblocks and struggles I sometimes face. It's approaching people with an "innocent until proven guilty" mindset and then offering forgiveness and mercy, even when the person is guilty. Mostly it's coming from a place of humility that grounds me back to the reality that these people are just like me—prone to failure, weak, and in need of grace.

I seek to see the whole person and remember that they have a backstory. I remember that maybe their dog threw up as they were running out the door in the morning or they spilled coffee on themselves on the drive over or they were just yelled at by a birth parent. I remember that so often they are overworked, overextended, and underpaid. I remember that always they carry their own stories and pains and weaknesses, and they are deeply loved by and precious to God.

Forgiveness

"Forgiving each other; as the Lord has forgiven you, so you also must forgive" (Colossians 3:13). My son was complaining about a girl in his class when he uttered the never-to-be-said word: "I *hate* her." *Gasp. We don't hate anyone.* I launched into my mama speech about hatred being like murder[2] and that if we hate people, we "cannot love God" (1 John 4:20). I gave him my best don't-you-dare-say-*hate*, Scripture-laced rebuke. I told him that I struggle to love some people too. My ten-year-old called from the back of the van, "You mean like Ms. Catherine?" Oof. Yes, like her.

Ms. Catherine is a worker who wounded me and my family so deeply that I certainly have held hatred for her in my heart at times. Not just "not love." Hatred. To the point where my ten-year-old can see through my "We should love everyone" facade and knows exactly where my heart is.

Many of you carry your own wounds and trials caused by workers. I've sat with foster parents who carry tales of lies and betrayals, failures and inadequacies. The wrongs can rob you of the trust you once had in others and steal the joy you once experienced as a foster parent. And because they are legitimately wrong, they can also tempt you to feel justified in your "not love." What if you called your lack of love what the Bible calls it? Is it hatred, bitterness, self-righteousness, anger? Don't write off your struggle as a general negative feeling toward "the system." When we call sin what it is, we are able to find freedom and forgiveness. We don't have to be controlled by bitterness and anger. It has been paid for at the cross.[3] When we confess and repent, we can experience forgiveness for where our hearts have gone wrong and extend forgiveness to our workers for their wrongs. We can pray to our Father, "Forgive us our trespasses, as we forgive them that trespass against us" (Matthew 6:12 NMB).

Love

"Put on love" (*Colossians 3:14*). Forgiveness leaves a vacuum. It provides a clean slate. But in my experience, *clean* is another word for "not yet dirty again." The "negative" we felt before needs to be replaced with something else. This revisits the idea we saw in chapter 6 and in Ephesians 4 of "putting off" and "putting on." I put off bitterness, and I put on compassion. I put off self-righteousness, and I put on humility. I put off anger, and I put on patience. I put off hatred, and I put on love.

Love is not an emotion. It is an action. It can be chosen, decided, *put on*. Love does not have to be felt; it can be placed on like a cloak, covering the ugly that may still linger underneath. The beauty of this covering is that it's not like a mask. It doesn't simply hide and fake. It transforms. Putting on love is the first step to *becoming* loving. I fake it 'til I make it not because I'm fake but because I'm committed to—by the Holy Spirit's empowering strength—"making it" to the goal of truly loving.

I highly doubt that when your worker shows up at your door, your heart is overwhelmed with affection as you think, *I love you so much*. But what does it look like to love your worker? I present to you "1 Corinthians 13: A Foster Parent and Worker Love Story":

Love is patient. When you call him and he doesn't call you back, are you patient? Are you understanding? Are you long-suffering as the Lord has been with you?

Love is kind. When she makes a mistake and you have a choice of how you're going to talk to her about it, do you choose warmth and gentleness? Is your perspective generous and charitable?

It does not envy or boast; it is not arrogant. Love doesn't think we're better than them. It doesn't come with, *What is wrong with them? Why can't they just do what they said they were going to do? Why can't they do their job right?* It comes with humility and understanding.

It is not rude. Are you demanding? Disrespectful? Disagreeable?

It does not insist on its own way. Are you faulting them for being inflexible, not hearing your voice, not valuing your perspective, when you're actually doing those things yourself?

It is not irritable. Are you easily bothered, easily angered, easily offended? *Ugh, she was twenty minutes late again!* Are you forbearing, or are you often irritated?

It is not resentful. The NIV phrases this "Love . . . keeps no record of wrongs." Do you have a mental list of all the short-comings, a resentful tally of every wrongdoing?

It does not rejoice at wrongdoing, but rejoices with the truth. Sometimes the failures of our workers help build our case for how broken the system is, how wronged we and our kids are. Sometimes we revel in the one-upmanship of what a terrible worker we have when we share a part-solidarity, part-whining chat with another foster parent.

Love bears all things, believes all things, hopes all things, endures all things. Basically, love puts up with a lot. Love has a high threshold for people's weaknesses and mistakes. Love doesn't float downstream with the natural current of annoyances and provocations. It paddles hard, against the flow, toward forgiveness and understanding, toward charity and kindness.

Thankfulness

"And be thankful" (*Colossians 3:15*). Thank your workers often and specifically. And if those words made you laugh or roll your eyes or say, "But . . . ," then you probably need to hear them even more so. If your workers are doing their job well, thank them. Let them know that their work is important and it makes a difference, that you see it and are grateful. And if your workers aren't doing their jobs well, thank them all the more, because showing gratitude is about so much more than what it speaks to them.

The hidden—and maybe primary—effect of gratitude is the effect it has on your own heart. Search for the things—elusive as they may be—that you can thank God for. Scripture tells us to "give thanks in all circumstances" (1 Thessalonians 5:18), which means that, in fact, there is something to give thanks for in every single circumstance, and it will serve your heart to seek it out.

My grandmom (who was the OG foster mom of our family over *sixty years ago!*) is chronically ill and often in the hospital. But visit her there and ask how she's doing, and you'll hear much more about the kindness of God in providing a Christian nurse who encouraged her and a roommate to share the gospel with and a delivered-right-to-her-bed, hot, delicious meal than you will the pain that she's experiencing. She bleeds gratitude—even throughout situations that many of us would complain through—because she sees God's hand orchestrating everything for her good.

Grateful people aren't grateful because they have more to be grateful for; they're grateful because of the way they see the world. Gratitude means approaching life with humility and worship. When we know who we are and we remember what we deserve, it provokes our hearts to worship the God who has given us something so different.

The Bible doesn't provide a how-to for interacting with workers. These representatives of the system are more than just that; they are people. And God calls us, as *His* people, to compassion, kindness, forgiveness, love, and gratitude.

Admittedly, this chapter has been more about coping with workers than improving the situation with them, but that's not to say there aren't things you could and should be doing to improve your situation. If I were sitting across from you, I'd have a whole list of ideas for practically navigating the system and advocating for your children. I'd probably say things like, "You can't let them treat you like that," and "You need to call this person instead." But that's not what this book is. This book isn't advice for foster parents; it's *truth* for foster parents. Advice may not apply to every situation, may not work even if it did, but truth from God's Word is always for you, all the time. Even when you're not sure what to do, His Word directs us in *how* we are to do it.

I've called supervisors and written letters to judges and cc'd *all* the people. I've taken steps to advocate for myself and my children. And I've learned that the principles above—of kindness and compassion and gratitude—are the most important part of doing it all. Communicate what you and your children need, and do it with strength and conviction and perseverance. But remember that "gracious words are like a honeycomb" (Proverbs 16:24), and you know what they say about catching flies. Be flexible and easygoing, approach with humility and respect, speak with kindness and appreciation. And wrap up this marriage of strength and humility in a covering of prayer, an acknowledgment that while you're speaking up and stepping out, you're ultimately trusting God.

Get off the Roller Coaster

Foster care is a roller coaster, right? We can all agree on that. But the longer I'm at this, the more I'm learning that I don't always have to go along for the ride. Yeah, there are ups and downs and "thrown-for-a-loops" that are unavoidable. But the dreadful, stomach-turning, "Get me off this thing!" anticipation and whiplash of every bump in the path? I've stepped out of line, child in hand, and I don't do it anymore.

There have been countless times that I've received devastating news from a worker that—in typical roller-coaster fashion— was soon undone. "Oh, actually, this thing that was supposed to happen isn't happening, and this other, very different thing is going to happen instead." Details emerge, goals change, people show up and leave. Giving the benefit of the doubt, I can only believe that these workers are doing their best with the information they have. But I don't need to go along for all the ups and downs as the information changes and changes again.

I can cast all my cares on God because He cares for me.[4] I can give up carrying around my anxieties and trade them for a deep trust in the goodness and sovereignty of God. Jumping off the roller coaster isn't just about that though. It's also about getting wise to the system. When you realize that half the things you worry about never happen and half the things you'd never think to worry about do, you learn that all the worrying is just a big waste. It's like a modern-day child-welfare boy who cried wolf. I'm not calling any one person the lying boy; I'm just pointing out that you learn to stop believing the cries. You learn not to worry about tomorrow, "for tomorrow will worry about itself" (Matthew 6:34 NIV).

My current foster daughter was recently switched to the adoption unit. After a year, her goal was changed from reunification to adoption. Afterward my husband said, "Wow, that went fast." Of course, it wasn't any faster than our other kids' cases, but it *felt* much faster. With our first daughter's adoption, our focus on the direction of the case was all-consuming. We held our breath between appointments with the worker, waited for a report after every visit, held on to every possibility that was spoken, counted down to every court date, spent court days pacing and worrying, checked our phones constantly, talked and worried, thought about and focused on the next checkpoint. It made for the longest 27.5 months of my life. This time around, we put our energy into loving our girl and supporting her mom, and it magically went fast.

The worry and fear and anger I've experienced in the past as I've ridden every up and down of the roller coaster have brought me nothing. So now? I still approach foster parenting with my whole self, but I don't focus on the what-ifs I hear from workers, the back-and-forth of information and misinformation. Those used to jerk me left and right and upside down, but now

I choose to sit them out. I watch them play out from afar and stay steady on the ground.

My friend Sandy ended up adopting the children—the ones the division lied about—from the story at the beginning of this chapter. And her story might just be the perfect way to start and end this chapter. At the beginning, gross mishandling and deception. And at the end, redemption and adoption and forever family. But it's not the happily ever after that I want to point you to. It's the messy middle.

"It was life shattering. We lamented, regretted, and grumbled," Sandy said. "Did we trust? Did we cry out, 'Lord help us in our unbelief'? Sadly, no. We blamed and rehearsed all the reasons why we couldn't."

There was no step Sandy could have made to fix this situation. There was no simple way to make this right, and she couldn't just advocate her way out of it. Like so many of the situations we all face with our workers, she was left with very little to *do*, and so she was driven instead to turn to God.

She shared, "The Spirit did a mighty work on our hearts. Jesus often works through the deepest valleys of pain to bring beauty from ashes. Through many prayers, struggles, and hardships, Jesus turned our fear into faith. This too was *life shattering*. We embraced His plan, not ours. Life is busy and challenging but very rewarding, and we know now that God has us right where He wants us to be."

What better way to end this chapter than with a reminder that throughout the missteps and despite the damage done, God has a good plan. Our lives can be shattered by the wrongs and mistakes of others, but they can also be shattered—in the best way possible, in a way that actually puts them back together—by the realities of God's presence within those hardships. Our God is above and throughout every step and misstep of every worker we come across, working them all to accomplish His very good plan. I know this system and its workers may fail my children. But also, "I know that [God] can do all things, and that no purpose of [his] can be thwarted" (Job 42:2).

*A note to any "workers" reading this: You are "overhearing" a heart-to-heart between foster parents. This chapter isn't meant to discourage you; it's only meant to validate the experience that, sadly, many foster parents have had to walk through. I want to say, for the record, that I think you have the most important job in the world. And when it's done well, it's absolutely world-changing. The work you do protects children, supports families, and brings healing. The way you're expected to do it—too many kids, too many visits, too much paperwork, not enough time—is unfair and unrealistic, and we'd all struggle under the burden of it. Thank you for the work you do. Thank you for the times you show up with love for our children, compassion toward their parents, and understanding for us. Your faithful—and too often thankless—work does not ultimately go unnoticed. I hope that the foster parents you serve thank you often and heartily, but if they don't, hear it from me: Thank you for all you do. More importantly, your work is always seen by God Himself, and He will one day reward and honor you for a job "well done" (Matthew 25:23).

fifteen

Foster-Caring Community

A group of foster mom friends sat in my living room. We snacked on ten different variations of chocolate and drank three different variations of sangria and talked about life and foster care and this very book you're reading now. They're the women I've approached with questions and tears as I've struggled as a foster parent, and I wanted you to benefit from their wisdom as I have.

"*Yes! Me too! I totally agree! I understand!*" peppered our conversation throughout the night, as well as "*I would never say this to anyone else,*" and "*No one else would get this.*" And as we experienced the power of togetherness and like-mindedness, I decided—then and there—that this book needed a chapter on community.

Nothing is quite like this upside-down world of parenting other people's children. We live in hellos and goodbyes and victories and heartbreaks, addiction and trauma and diagnoses and neglect. Because there is so much to explain and so few who understand, living this life alone can be awfully lonely.

We Need Each Other

Our need for other people is written in our DNA, and God highlights that need all throughout His Word. We see it in the first pages of Scripture when God created the first person and immediately said, "It is not good that the man should be alone" (Genesis 2:18). We see it in the New Testament when God's people lived in a caring, generous community and walked out all the "one anothers" together.[1] If you're paying attention to God's Word, you can't miss His heart for living life together.

Community is a rich picture of how life can be lived in togetherness. It's about far more than proximity or a collection of people. Community is about shared mission and vision, about a common goal and a commitment to others within the community. Simply put, community is about relationship and partnership.

Relationship is joy that togetherness brings to the journey. It's carrying each other and leaning against each other. It's the camaraderie of getting to do this life together and the relief of learning that you're not crazy. It's having someone to laugh with and cry with.

Partnership is all that we bring to each other. It's the idea that we can do more and we can do better because we're together. It's the service we bring each other that empowers us to be able to do all that needs to be done. It's the information we share to know and do better. It's the emotional strength we provide each other, the prayers we bring for each other that infuse us with strength we wouldn't otherwise have.

When we work together in community, in relationship and partnership, we get a taste of the wholeness of relationships that God intended for us.

What If I Don't Have It?

Before I go too deeply into how important community is, I want to speak to those who don't have it. I've spoken to many around the country who feel alone in their foster care journey and don't know what to do. Unfortunately, it's not always within our power to create community, but that doesn't mean we're completely powerless to pursue it.

Use It

Don't discount the community that already surrounds you just because they don't understand your experience as a foster parent. Here's the secret: Everyone is struggling. Your people may not be struggling through the same things you're struggling through, but it doesn't mean they don't understand the struggle. It's all "common to man" (1 Corinthians 10:13), after all. The experiences and trials they've walked through and the encouragement and truth they've learned all hold lessons from which you can benefit. Let the people who already love you serve as your foster care community and provide encouragement and service and care.

Be patient with your friends and family as they grow in their understanding of foster care and how to serve you as a foster parent. Remember, *we* signed up for this, and we signed up our people for it along with us whether they like it or not. Show mercy for their lack of support or understanding, their awkward questions or bumbling words. Teach and correct when appropriate; overlook and love often. We need to be understanding of those who are along for the ride that we've put them on.

Create It

I created a formal support group for foster moms in my area because I love start-ups and projects. But you don't have to be an extroverted party person to create community. Maybe for you it's much simpler. Launch a Facebook group for local foster parents, initiate a text chain or book study, host a playgroup or dessert night. It might be as simple as getting to know one other foster parent and striking up a friendship. Don't sit back and wait for community; look for ways to create it.

Join It

Chances are there is some sort of support group, training, or get-together in your area, maybe through the state, your agency, or a local church ministry. Search for it, then take a deep breath and show up and join. I know it's awkward, but become convinced and then be compelled. The benefits trump the awkwardness, and the fruit will be worth that first hard step.

Most of the Scripture referenced in this chapter was written to believers within the context of a local church. The church is God's primary plan for His people to be taught and encouraged and served.[2] So much so that the image He provides is of "one body in Christ, and individually members one of another" (Romans 12:5). If you are not involved in a local body of believers, then you are missing out on a large part of God's design for you to experience community. Start here. Even if you don't share the common identity of foster parenting with your church family members, you share the most important identity of child and follower of God.

Force It

When I became a foster parent, I knew exactly one foster mom. She was twice my age, and we had nothing in common. I walked up to her and said, "I'm becoming a foster parent. Will you be my friend?" And that's exactly what she has become. I've gone to her with questions and issues for seven years now. She's still much older than I am, we still have little in common, but we share the common ground of foster care, and that has bonded us.

Ask for It

Foster parenting is frontline mission work. Caring for vulnerable children and families hands-on should be supported and served by our families, communities, and churches. Ideally, those surrounding us would automatically step up and provide babysitting, meals, and other practical help, but there's a good chance they won't. They may not know how to help or even realize you need it; they may not have a vision for how serving you is actually a way to serve vulnerable children. It can feel strange to ask people to serve us, but it's actually a holy request. First, it's a practice in humility for us. Asking for help reveals our weakness and opens us up to receive grace—from God, through the simple exchange God promises of humility for grace,[3] and from others, through their tangible service. Second, it's empowering for others. Asking for help from others provides them with the privilege and gift of *getting* to be involved in practically serving the vulnerable. When we operate in self-sufficient pride, we steal the opportunity from those around us to get involved in the sacrificial mission of foster care.

Google It

As much as face-to-face, real-life relationships are important—and they are!—if you don't have people around you who have the experience and information you need, you have the twenty-first-century gift of access to millions of people around the world who do! I met a group of some of my closest friends—women who know me well, who carry me and encourage me and challenge me—on Facebook. We text daily. We even vacationed together last year! These are real and deep friendships that have changed my life. Facebook, Instagram, email, and blogs are gifts from God that can be sources of stand-in encouragement and community.

Secret Handshakes

Healthy community is defined by give-and-take. I like to picture my friendships in three categories, my hands extending in invitation in three different ways—reaching up, reaching out, and linking arms. When I can identify people who fit into all three groups, I know that I'm pursuing relationships in which I'm both serving and being served.

I have a lot to learn, and I want relationships in which I'm in the learner's seat. These "reaching up" relationships are often with people who are older and have more experience and wisdom. Like Paul's encouragement to "follow my example, as I follow the example of Christ" (1 Corinthians 11:1 NIV), we seek out people who can teach and lead us. It could be a formal mentor relationship, or it could just be a friend who is further ahead in their journey and becomes your go-to for input and advice. My friend Jesse has been a foster parent for a few years longer than I have and has cared for almost twice as many kids. I trust her opinion and experience more than almost anyone's, and I often seek out her wisdom and input.

When I became a foster parent, I didn't have one easy, natural relationship with another foster parent. I did my best, but I just stumbled along and figured things out on my own. As I gained experience, I became passionate about other foster parents not having to struggle and stumble as I had. I pursued "reaching out" relationships with those who were new to foster care and might need someone to whom they could bring their questions or struggles or tears. As friends and acquaintances delved into foster care, I would write a note or bring a meal and let them know "I'm here. Please reach out if you need me." Following the Titus 2 principle of teaching and urging the young men and women, we should be pursuing relationships with those whom we may be able to train and encourage.

The people we "link arms" with are the ones we do life with. Simply put, they're our friends, our people, our "one anothers."

One Anothers

I already mentioned the high priority God places on living life together, especially in the New Testament's "one anothers." The New Testament has one hundred references about how we should relate to one another as fellow Christians.[4] Here are a few.

Encourage and Build Up

"Therefore encourage one another and build one another up" (1 Thessalonians 5:11). Our words hold great power. They carry the ability to bring hope and life and change. Words of encouragement can be spoken softly across cups of coffee or hastily texted through a screen—the power is in the truth they bring. Romans 1:12 calls this being "mutually encouraged by each other's faith." The greatest gifts my friends give me are their words. And nothing is more helpful than when they serve as pointers, reminding me of the truth and hope of the gospel.

Serve

"Serve one another humbly in love" (Galatians 5:13 NIV).
My sister-in-law and fellow foster and adoptive mom, Jayme,
has served me more than any other friend. I can't list or even
remember all the times, but I can name a few. Like the time I
was sick in bed and I heard her downstairs ushering my kids
to her car without me even asking. Or the time we all got lice
from a foster child and she spent five hours picking bugs out
of our heads. Or the many times she has dropped chocolate
or sushi or beer on my doorstep with a "Thanks for how well
you loved" note when a child has gone home.

Welcome

*"Therefore welcome one another as Christ has welcomed
you, for the glory of God" (Romans 15:7).* There should be
no place other foster parents feel more welcome than in our
presence. May parents feel free to come with their chaos, their
children's behavioral struggles, their own emotional ups and
downs. May parents never feel like they have to apologize for
or explain their children's needs. *You are welcome here with
your mess. We bring our own messes, but we'll do our best to
serve and encourage you in yours!*

Spur On

*"Let us consider how we may spur one another on toward
love and good deeds" (Hebrews 10:24 NIV).* When my big kids
were babies, my best friends and I got together one to three
times a week for the most uniquely beautiful time of fellowship and community affectionately known as "playgroup."
We talked about breastfeeding and sleep schedules and the
color of our kids' poop. But you know what else we talked

about? We talked about living radically, serving sacrificially, and giving generously. And we talked *a lot* about foster care and adoption.

Last year one of the friends texted the group of the seven of us a picture of her new foster son with the caption: "You guys! All seven of us are foster and adoptive moms now!" When we were having playgroup eight years ago, we were just talking as friends, sharing our burdens, relating things we were learning in Scripture. Through our time together, God birthed in all of us a passion for vulnerable children, a desire to bring them into our homes and serve their families, a heart for adoption. As we spent time together, we spurred each other on toward love and good deeds.

Meet

"Not giving up meeting together . . . but encouraging one another" (Hebrews 10:25 NIV). Meeting together can be difficult. Busy schedules and struggling kids can make it feel impossible. But it is not impossible. Don't give up. I met friends the other night at 8:45 p.m. We made a date and stuck to it because even though we were tired and our time together was short, we were convinced that we really needed each other.

When possible, involve your kids in your foster care community. It's important for all our kids—biological, adopted, foster—to be with other kids who share similar experiences and stories. Having an understanding community where they don't have to explain their story or role is a privilege for them. There, our biological children can speak of their confusion and loss. There, our foster and adopted children can be with other children who carry the same experiences as them, who understand their past histories and present struggles.

Teach and Admonish

"Let the word of Christ dwell in you richly, teaching and admonishing one another in all wisdom" (Colossians 3:16). Sometimes I need to be encouraged, and sometimes I need to be straight-up admonished. Sometimes I need my friends to cry with me and hold my hand, and sometimes I need them to look me in the face and say, "You're being selfish. Get over yourself." I've experienced the faithful wounds of a friend,[5] and they are sweet. We need to have friends who love us so much and are so committed to our good that they are willing to bring us truth and correction, even when it's hard.

Confess

"Confess your sins to one another" (James 5:16). Soon after adopting her daughter from India, my best friend Amy faced an unexpected struggle. I sat with her as she talked about feeling prepared for the "normal" post-adoption issues—attachment and fears and delays—but being completely taken off guard by the struggle she herself was facing in experiencing anger toward her newly adopted daughter. She humbly confessed, "I'm angry and I'm harsh and I'm terrified I'm going to ruin her." I watched the guilt and fear melt from her face as I confided, "I struggle with the same exact thing." She looked with hope to another friend, another foster and adoptive mom, who nodded in affirmation as she asked, "You do too?" A few weeks later, my friend shared that this moment was a turning point for her. Confession wasn't an incantation that made anger magically disappear. We shared no wisdom that supernaturally changed her heart. But this conversation was an invitation for grace, an opening of the mouth and the heart in humility and of the hands toward grace. My friend

simply experienced the divine formula of God giving grace to the humble.[6]

Our conversation, outside of the safety of other foster and adoptive parents, might have been difficult to navigate. With the "there's no difference" narrative surrounding our foster and adopted children, which is both completely true yet not, it can be hard to admit the ugliness of our own hearts as it relates to our kids. A community of understanding friends is a gift, but—with or without it—confession is a mandate. Do you need grace? Avail yourself of it through the gift of confession. "Humble yourselves, therefore, under the mighty hand of God so that at the proper time he may exalt you" (1 Peter 5:6) and you may experience the God who "gives more grace" (James 4:6).

Pray

"Pray for one another" (James 5:16). A friend of mine is walking through an extremely painful reunification of the nearly three-year-old son she has mothered since birth. When we talk, I feel completely helpless. She is experiencing fear and anger and utter heartbreak, and it feels like there's absolutely nothing I can do to intervene or even to comfort her. But as trite as it may feel, I am able to do the very best thing for her by bringing her and her son to the almighty God in prayer. Prayer isn't like saying, "I'm thinking of you." It's not a nice sentiment or a cute expression that we say to others to let them know we care. Prayer is the most powerful thing we can do for another person, the most loving action we can take. Reread chapter 4 if you need convincing. Prayer works.

Carry

"Carry each other's burdens" (Galatians 6:2 NIV). This verse brings to my mind never-ending text chains with friends.

Sometimes we're sending verses and encouragement; sometimes we're offering practical help. Mostly we're just jumping into the mess of it all, sitting there in friendship and carrying some of the burden. The stuff we carry as foster parents is heavy. Our hearts are weighed down with emotions and fears and struggles; our hands are full with all our responsibilities and the little lives we carry. We need someone to reach out to, someone we can unload on and say, "Do me a favor; carry this with me."

Love

"A new command I give you: Love one another. As I have loved you, so you must love one another" (John 13:34 NIV). We are to love one another the way Christ has loved us—that is, extravagantly and sacrificially, giving again and again, with no expectation of gain or return. What does Christlike love look like walked out in real life? It looks like all the "one anothers" listed above. Love looks like encouraging and serving and welcoming and carrying burdens. And this love isn't just motivated by a desire to be a good friend or to have good friends who reciprocate. It is motivated and empowered, prompted and brought to life by the love of Jesus. As His beloved, we become lovers.

Hold Up My Hands

Exodus might be the last place you'd think to look for encouragement for foster parents, but even Exodus has something for us, friends.

The people of God, the Israelites, were wandering the desert when the Amalekites attacked them from behind. But Moses had a plan: "Choose some of our men and go out to fight the Amalekites," he said to Joshua. "Tomorrow I will stand on top of the hill with the staff of God in my hands" (Exodus 17:9 NIV). And his plan worked. "As long as Moses held up his hands, the Israelites were winning, but whenever he lowered his hands, the Amalekites were winning" (v. 11 NIV). Moses had this important task of protecting God's people. No one else could wield this "staff of God" (v. 9 NIV) on his behalf. But he was weak, his "hands grew tired" (v. 12 NIV).

Why would God call Moses to something as important as protecting God's chosen people and then allow him to be overcome by his weakness? Actually, God provided exactly what Moses needed. When his "hands grew tired, they took a stone and put it under him and he sat on it. Aaron and Hur held his hands up—one on one side, one on the other—so that his hands remained steady till sunset" (v. 12 NIV). It seems Moses needed a dose of divine strength or supernatural willpower, but God provided exactly what Moses needed: people. People who stood with him when he was weak, who supported him and helped him accomplish what God had called him to do.

I don't know about you, but I see myself here in Moses. A biological parent accuses me, a worker lies to me, or my kids' behaviors confound me, and I'm left feeling under attack and battle worn. And as I wonder why God has called me to things that I don't feel equipped for, I am met by a supporting hand on the left and on the right. I am met by the people He has sent to help me. And the beauty in arriving at the place where I *just couldn't* without the others He brings along is that I'm led to worship Him for what *He* has done. I see the people surrounding me, who have held up my arms and fought my battles with me. Yes, it fills my heart with gratitude for them but so much more: It points my eyes to God—the One who brings victory.

sixteen

A Small-Time County Judge

Sometimes ignorance *is* bliss.

I was a new foster parent, desperate for any insider's tidbit I could get on the process. I knew I'd be seeing my friend who was a law guardian—the court-appointed legal representative of a foster child—at a birthday party soon. This friend practiced in my child's county, so not only did he understand the process; he knew the specific players and the way the game was played. When I arrived at the party, I played it super cool and immediately cornered and interrogated him. I asked him all the ins and outs of the process and then said, "Do you know Judge So-and-So?" I was eager to know anything about the man who held my precious child's life in his hands.

"He. Is. Crazy." Those three words spoken lightly with a small chuckle rooted fear deep in my heart. My friend continued with tales of the craziness: falling asleep during court, waking and yelling at the lawyers, completely erratic behavior. His final consensus: "Honestly, he could do anything." That was just enough to bend me up into the fetal position. This man—this "crazy" man—was the one determining the fate of this little girl, holding the cards, doling out the future. He sat, as judge, at the helm of this whole system that held her.

God Is the Judge

"Judge" is one of the titles God reserves for Himself. His Word names Him the righteous Judge and points to His judgment seat.[1] It reminds us that He will judge the world and that He loves justice.[2] Our God is the almighty and perfect Judge.

As a lover of justice, God calls His followers to pursue and love justice as well. He commands His people to "hold fast to love and justice" (Hosea 12:6), to "act justly" (Micah 6:8 NIV), and to "learn to do right; seek justice" (Isaiah 1:17 NIV). He calls us to live in and pursue what is right, and he "loves the just" (Psalm 37:28 NIV).

God loves justice and the just. But those He created bend and break and fall out of this order, and injustice seeps into everything. As foster parents, we see firsthand how foster care drips with injustice—toward the children, toward the biological family, toward us. We stand in the middle of this broken system appointed to *uphold* justice yet surrounded by what appears so unjust.

Appointed by God

Every judge takes an oath, a promise to "administer justice" and "do equal right" to all.[3] *So help them God.* Sometimes—when my anger over the injustice of it all bubbles to overflowing—I want to smack the hand off the Bible that the official swears on and hiss, "Leave God out of this!" Sometimes this system seems to me like justice gone awry, like a gaggle of rogue men and women wearing robes and issuing judgments, completely godless and utterly unjust.

But how dare I erase the sovereign King from my picture of the world He reigns over. "For there is no authority except from God, and those that exist have been instituted by God" (Romans 13:1). What I know about my God is that He does no wrong, He makes no mistakes, He—ultimately—allows no injustice to prevail. Yet He is the One who institutes authority, who has placed these judges on the benches on which they preside.

When we're met with a system so unjust, how are we to respond? Rebel and reject? March and rail against? *Maybe*.[4] There's a place for advocacy that fights against injustice and stands for righteousness. But for *most* of us, *most* of the time, we are to submit to the authorities that God has put in place. I am periodically contacted by advocacy groups who want me to rally for change in the child welfare system. But I've come to the conclusion that for me, for now, railing against the system and being a part of the system as a foster parent cannot coexist. I'm convinced that the way I can best affect the broken system is by participating in it and making my piece of it a little less broken.

So I follow court orders and I play by the rules and I go with the flow of this broken system. But it's not because I'm a respecter of the system itself. It's because I trust God. Nero was burning Christians when Paul encouraged the Roman church to "be subject to the governing authorities" (Romans 13:1). Jesus spoke to the man who was handing him over to be killed, "You would have no authority over me at all unless it had been given you from above" (John 19:11). The Sovereign One doles out authority to the "governing authorities"—namely, the judges in our kids' cases—to accomplish His will. So my following the system is ultimately following God.

We "submit" to the judge on the bench because of our "reverent fear of God" (1 Peter 2:18 NIV). We believe God has a good plan, even when it seems like those making the plans are not good. We say along with Job, "I know that you can do all things, and that no purpose of yours can be thwarted" (Job 42:2). This may provoke questions and cause confusion, but it ultimately leads me to a deeper faith in God as the just and sovereign King.

When my littles watch a movie, they get nervous about how things will turn out. During every tense situation, they look at me with fearful eyes and ask, "Are they going to be okay?" And all it takes is a nod from their mama and the assurance, "They're going to be okay," for them to rest easy again. The scary becomes less scary when you know that all is going to work out.

We know the ending of this story. God wins. Justice prevails. "For we know him who said, 'Vengeance is mine; I will repay'" (Hebrews 10:30). Right now we're stuck in the halfway mark of the pages, where things can seem hopeless and dim. We sit in broken spaces with hurting children. We see a system that continues to hurt them, and we see injustice winning. We cry out with the psalmist, "How long will the wicked triumph?" (Psalm 94:3 NKJV). But we know the answer: "God will bring into judgment both the righteous and the wicked, for there will be a time for every activity, a time to judge every deed" (Ecclesiastes 3:17 NIV). We may not see justice now, when we expect it, but we *will* see it.

Unjust Judge

Jesus was a storyteller. A writer myself, I love to think of Him this way. If anyone could rightly wear the cloak of "holier than thou," it would be Jesus. Instead, He spoke the language of the people and met them where they were. He approached them as Friend and Teacher. Parables are the perfect picture of this. Parables were Jesus's way of using storytelling to share truth about Himself in a way the people could relate to. I like to think that one parable—the one of the unjust judge—was placed in Scripture specifically for us, for foster parents, to read thousands of years later.

> And he told them a parable to the effect that they ought always to pray and not lose heart. He said, "In a certain city there was a judge who neither feared God nor respected man. And there was a widow in that city who kept coming to him and saying, 'Give me justice against my adversary.' For a while he refused, but afterward he said to himself, 'Though I neither fear God nor respect man, yet because this widow keeps bothering me, I will give her justice, so that she will not beat me down by her continual coming.'" (Luke 18:1–5)

Scripture spells out the lesson before even telling the story: "They ought always to pray and not lose heart" (v. 1). Jesus wove this tale of an unjust judge so that when we face hardships— say, for example, when we face an unjust judge in our child's case—we will remember to pray and not lose heart. What a perfect memory-association trick: when we see injustice prevailing, we're to remember Jesus's words and, rather than raise our hands in defeat, fall to our knees in prayer. God allows injustice for many reasons that we may never understand, but certainly one is to bring us back to dependence on Him as the Great Judge and lead us to plead for justice in prayer.

Prayer is not a fool's errand, as it may sometimes seem. In some confusing and divinely perfect plan, our prayers have been determined by God to accomplish His will. Read what Jesus mercifully teaches His followers at the conclusion of this parable: "And the Lord said, 'Hear what the unrighteous judge says. And *will not God give justice to his elect*, who cry to him day and night? Will he delay long over them? I tell you, *he will give justice to them speedily*'" (vv. 6–8, emphasis mine).

My definition of *speedily* differs from God's. With the reference point of my thirty-seven years on earth, I think *speedily* means "now." But for the Alpha-and-Omega, Beginning-and-End, eternal God of forever past and future, "speedily" might not quite match my timeline. God answers His people's prayers for justice. Absolutely. "He *will* give justice to them" (v. 8, emphasis mine). But remember that our understanding of speed may not match His. We can hold prayers for justice with great faith, in complete confidence that He will answer them, but we hold them also in humble submission to His reign over time.

Small-Time County Judge

Oh, how I wish my eyes worked differently. I wish they weren't so consumed with the seen. I wish they were able to look past the obvious to the unseen realm of what is actually going on. Because what my law guardian friend drew my attention to was simply the *seen* part of the courtroom drama, when behind the scenes is where the real action is.

Who was *actually* holding my precious girl's fate in His hands? Not a judge, no human at all. It was the Lord. "For the LORD is our judge; the LORD is our lawgiver; the LORD is our king" (Isaiah 33:22). And the same Lord who held my little girl also held the heart of the judge himself. Proverbs 21:1 reminds us, "The king's heart is a stream of water in the hand of the LORD; he turns it wherever he will." If God controlled the hearts of the great ancient kings, we know that He also "turns wherever he will" the heart of a small-time county judge. I once pictured a great marble courtroom, just like in the movies. A man or woman who had never met me or my foster child, who was meant to uphold justice in a system so unjust, sat on a raised maple bench with a gavel, ready to determine my family's fate. Scowling while they listened to snippets of passed-on and incomplete facts, the judge made their decision, spewed their answer as the final authority. And we were left simply to live by their word.

But a new picture has taken over my heart. When a court date approaches and I'm tempted to worry that the worker won't communicate clearly, the advocate won't advocate correctly, and the judge will rule unjustly, I look past the players to the One directing the scene. This earthly judge who "holds all the power" is merely a county family court judge, while God—the King of the universe, the great Judge—is holding his heart, directing it, leading it exactly where He has planned for it to go. The image has come into focus. It doesn't all hinge on the failed person sitting on the center bench. It hinges on the One above, directing everything in perfect wisdom and love.

The Witness Stand

The waiting room is a cast of characters, for sure. A woman dressed in pajamas slouches back in the plastic seat and leans her head against the wall. A voice from down the hall grows louder and closer until the four officers hovering around the main desk spring into action and surround it. A man two seats from me whispers into his phone, somehow twisting the same four-letter word into an adjective, noun, and verb in the same sentence. A clerk opens the door and calls my foster daughter's name.

I walk into the courtroom and take my place across from the judge, behind the table of lawyers, an outsider to the decisions being made. The judge speaks with a rote sternness to all, barely lifting his eyes above the rim of his glasses. He calls me to my feet, just a few feet from my daughter's handcuffed father, inches from her weeping mother. I—all of a sudden—forget what hands are supposed to do; one squeezing the other tightly, trying to hold all of me together. I will a fake smile onto my lips as tears pool at my lashes. When my mouth finally opens, my voice reveals a foreign quavering, a pubescent thirteen-year-old-boy kind of cracking.

Not sure where to look—*by all means possible, avoid the eyes of the heartbroken parents as I break their hearts with my words just a little bit more*—I lock eyes with the judge. His face softens. It meets me with warmth and invites me to speak. He smiles as he listens to my girl's milestones, turns his head to the side in soft agreement when I share my heart for her and for her family. And I think at once, *He's on our side.* Now, I'm not talking "choose us to be her parents" kind of "our side." I'm talking *our* side, mine and my family's, the biological parents', our daughter's. I'm talking about the side of what is right, the side of justice.

I haven't felt this way about every judge before, certainly, but I did today. In this moment, I was reminded again that God is on our side. He sits on the throne as God Almighty, on the bench as the Holy Judge of All, but also, He is my Father. He is both ruling on high and close to His beloved. He is at once directing the judge's heart and holding mine. And He invites me to trust Him as He leads the heart of the judge, to pray that He would bring about what is good and right, and to remember that always, eventually, He brings justice.

seventeen

Foster Care Is Heartbreak

My brother just texted with news that we all were expecting but no one was ready for. After one year, the sweet baby boy they brought home from the hospital—their foster son, my nephew—is going home. Nausea bubbles into my throat as I imagine how they're feeling. Not imagine, *remember*. I don't have to imagine. I know this pain of goodbye well.

My brother handles things differently than I do. He wants people and fun and distractions; I prefer Netflix and cake and blanket cocoons. But the feeling is the same. "The reality is kicking in, and it's almost unbearable. It almost feels like our kid is dying and there's nothing we can do to save him. Really helpless, awful feeling. We're all crying on and off," his text reads.

There isn't a box to check for this kind of loss. The loss of someone who goes on living, just without you. It feels like a death. You lose "your" child, for goodness' sake. This little life that was dependent on you for every physical need, for nurturing—for life—is, in a moment, gone. Or maybe it's not like death. My friend Kessie says it's more like a missing child.

You know they're out there in the world, living without you, but you're unable to be with them, protect them, know that they're okay—unable to hold on to peace or experience whatever closure is supposed to be.[1]

It doesn't matter that this is what you signed up for, that this is "the job." You can know a sadness is coming and feel it just the same. You can want reunification to happen and still suffer the pain of it. My brother and sister-in-law could be the poster children for pro-reunification foster parenting—unlimited visits *at their house*, Christmas at bio Mom's with gifts for every member of the family. They have loved Mom well, made every effort to bring reunification about, and are still in absolute anguish. You can work toward something, pray for something, and still grieve that thing. You can believe a child should be with their parents, feel the joy of a family being made whole, and still carry the deep heartbreak of loss.

When we foster well, we step into more than just a role of caretaker, chef, tutor, landlord. We take on the role of parent and with it, often, the emotions that parents feel toward their children. It's only natural when we love deeply to also deeply experience the pain of loss.

And of course, saying goodbye isn't the only form of heartbreak. The breaking starts right at the beginning and follows through every step of this sad path. In just the past few days, I've had heartbreaking conversations with foster parents whose former, reunified foster children are on the brink of entering the system again, a mom whose adopted son committed suicide a few months ago, parents who are caring for their former foster son as his mom reenters rehab, a friend who had to call a DCF referral on a new mother with intellectual disabilities who can't care for her baby, a mom whose foster son was removed by the police after his violent outburst, an adoptive mom who is pursuing a fetal alcohol syndrome diagnosis for her daughter after months of significant behavioral struggles, a single mom whose foster son was reunified after two years and who finds herself a childless mother, a woman who was raped and is pregnant and searching for a family to care for her unborn daughter, a foster mom whose son has been transitioning back to his family for a painfully drawn-out six-month period. Every part of foster parenting and every person involved is affected by the heartbreak of it—before and after and all throughout. Foster care is initiated and touched by heartbreak through every single step.

How Did You Deal?

My friend Carley and I sat and talked about the loss she experienced a couple of years ago when she said goodbye to her foster son after nineteen months. "How did you deal?" I asked. I wanted her to outline a step-by-step plan of how to dig out of the sadness. If only it were that simple.

"You mean, how *am* I dealing?" she answered with a sad smile.

There isn't ever a quick once-and-done method for dealing with loss. But if I want to continue this mission of foster care, I need to learn how to be dealing with the heartbreak of it. Maybe not being okay but certainly becoming okay.

Remember to Prepare

I often receive messages from foster parents that go something like this: "My foster child is leaving next week. How do I prepare for this?" My stomach drops every time, and I think, *Oh, friend, if you're just beginning to prepare, you're in trouble.* Preparing your heart to say goodbye to a child begins the moment that child arrives. It's in how we think about them and how we plan, the way we consider the future, and how we view the family. We actively align our hearts and minds to many of the other truths in this book—about the family and the system and the God above it all—each day of this journey, not just before a goodbye.

Remember the Good

Consider both the memories you have and the impact you've had.

You might throw this book across the room, but I'm going to quote Tennyson anyway: "'Tis better to have loved and lost than never to have loved at all."[2] Would you ever opt out of the great joy of knowing and parenting the child you lost to protect yourself from the pain? Would you trade your memories for comfort? Maybe you're wallowing deep in heartbreak right now, and a resounding *Yes!* is your internal scream. Friend, take it from someone who once carried the great weight of heartbreak and is now accompanied by only the shadow of it: It gets better. The load gets lighter, the burden easier to carry, the moments of pain fewer and farther between. Memories have a way of fading from deep suffering to sweet sadness to contented joy. You were granted the great privilege of knowing and loving the child you lost. Remember with gratitude, even if the remembrance is still colored by pain. Your memories will become sweeter with each passing day.

Along with the memories, you also carry the gratification of the impact you've made. Every day a child has spent in your home is marked by your influence and participation in their heal-ing and growth. When my best friend Julie made the difficult de-cision to disrupt a placement and have a child moved to a home that was better suited to care for his significant needs (something

I've watched many amazing, loving, godly foster parents have to do, by the way), she felt like a failure. She questioned why God even brought this child into her home if it wasn't the right place for him. Then she made a list of all that she was able to do to serve this little boy that would continue to positively affect his life: enrolling him in school, getting him into therapy, pursuing a diagnosis for a genetic condition, identifying an allergy, getting treatment for his rotting teeth, advocating for him to be placed in the right home. In the midst of the guilt and sadness she was experiencing, she found great comfort in the important role God had for her in the time she cared for him. Make a list of your impact, your example, the love you showed, and the progress the child made. Remind yourself that it was not in vain. In every case, your heartbreak is the remnant of a job well done.

Remember Your God

The presence of a friend provides great comfort. What says friendship better than someone who shows up to sit with you in your sadness? Well, "there is a friend who sticks closer than a brother" (Proverbs 18:24). He is "near to the brokenhearted" (Psalm 34:18), and He puts your tears in His bottle.[3] So, in my sadness, I remember that He is near, and I cry to Him, "My soul is weary with sorrow; strengthen me according to your word" (Psalm 119:28 NIV).

And this same God is not only with me, He is also with the once-my-child whom I miss. So when my heart is filled with sadness, I do the only and best thing I can do: I pray to the One who is with my child still, the One who will be with my child always. While our loss may feel like a death, as my mom answered my brother's desperate text, "He is not dead. He is very much alive. And I will be praying for him every day for as long as he lives."

Remember There Is an End

Both of us stood with tears welling in our eyes. We were talking about walking through grief in a healthy way—something neither of us had been very good at but both were working toward.

"I'm learning that there are some things that may always bring a tear to my eye," my friend intimated with a contented sadness.

"Yes, we may carry the sadness forever," I agreed. "But not *forever* forever."

She understood and smiled. We both smiled.

There *will* be an end to every sadness, an expiration of every pain. One day our tears will be wiped away by God Himself. The griefs we carried through our days will be dissipated. The joy of understanding God's plan will melt our sadness into informed and comforted worship. These griefs of ours are light and momentary and are achieving for us eternal glory, and these sufferings are not worth comparing with that glory.[4]

I've rarely experienced the heartbreak of goodbye on its own. Typically tangled up with my pain are other difficult feelings as well: anxiety and fear, judgment, anger over injustice, disappointment and resentment. In day-to-day life, I usually handle tangled up knots in one of two ways: scissors or the trash can. Yesterday I cut through a rope the kids were playing with after about thirty seconds of trying to untangle it. The day before, I threw away a necklace after simply seeing a knot in the chain. I'll choose the shortcut, or I'll give up completely. I don't like the difficult work of trudging through hard things, and I'll always opt out or rush through when possible.

I've had to learn that spending time untangling the threads and processing through each of them serves my soul well. My fear needs the comforting truths of God's Word. My anger over injustice needs to be reminded that my God is just and will always bring justice in His time. My judgment needs to be confessed and repented of and needs the power of the gospel to transform. And my emotions need to be felt and experienced, walked through or crawled through or sat in, but not rushed by.

Grief doesn't allow shortcuts. It demands that you do your time, so to speak. In the past, my grief process looked like one day of lying on the couch, watching TV and eating too much bread, and the next day making a call to every worker in the tri-county area, letting them know that I had an opening in my home. I took the tasks of grieving as a checklist and challenge to race through to the end. But there is no skipping steps. It's like those poor kids on that stupid bear hunt: You can't go over it. You can't go under it. You've got to go through it.[5] The steps have a way of coming back around on you, revisiting and recycling until you've given them their proper space. We must learn to befriend our grief.

Now, maybe you're reading this and it's not resonating with you. Surprise! Not every person feels the same way about every experience. I sat in a room with fifteen foster moms and asked if any of them didn't feel heartbroken when a foster child left. They were my friends, and I knew the answer; it was why I asked. Two of them—two of my mentors, two of the most loving moms and best foster parents I know—shrugged their shoulders and raised their hands. "Yeah, I don't." If you've struggled with the guilt of not feeling heartbroken when a child leaves, I want you to read that again. You are not alone; many other foster parents feel just the same.

My friend Jesse explains it like this: "They drop these kids off, and they're strangers to you. You have no prior connection, no information, and you're not going to just feel an automatic, supernatural love for every kid who walks through your door." I've had friends share the deep shame and guilt they feel when they're relieved that a child leaves, the loneliness they feel at not sharing in the grief that their many foster parent friends seem to experience. Everyone's experience is different and everyone's feelings will be different. If this chapter doesn't apply to you, there is no shame, no condemnation. If you've served and cared for your foster child well—even while lacking the feelings of love—then you *have* loved "in deed and in truth" (1 John 3:18).

Job and Grief

I'm currently reading the book of Job, and what better friend could there be to serve as a guide through grief? If you've never read Job, here's a drive-by synopsis: Job was "blameless and upright" (Job 1:1), a man whom God regarded as a trophy of faithful servanthood. God and Satan are discussing him when Satan has a wily plan: strike down the faithful Job and prove that he's faithful only because of all that God has given him. God accepts, willingly allowing His faithful follower to be inflicted with every form of sadness—not because He has to make a deal with the devil to prove Himself, and not because He doesn't love Job, but because He has a beautiful plan to glorify Himself to Job (and to the rest of us who read along with Job's story still). In Job 1 and 2, Job loses everything—all his children, all his wealth, and his health. The next forty-one chapters walk us through his grief process, including some advice from unhelpful friends, a shocking back-and-forth with God, and Job's ultimate restoration. This book's exploration of the suffering of man and of the wrestling with God that follows such suffering holds lessons for us in our grief.

Naked I Came

Job's servants find him and bring him bad news after bad news. "Then Job arose and *tore his robe* and *shaved his head* and fell on the ground and *worshiped*. And he said, 'Naked I came from my mother's womb, and naked shall I return. The LORD gave, and the LORD has taken away; *blessed be the name of the LORD.*' In all this Job did not sin or charge God with wrong" (1:20–22, emphasis mine).

Job is faced with overwhelming loss and sadness. His reaction is appropriate. He rips his clothes in an act of grief, shaves his head in an act of grief, and then—in seeming contradiction to those two grief-filled actions—falls to his knees in an act of worship. He blesses the name of the Lord and acknowledges that everything he had and lost was a gift from God to begin with.

What an extraordinary picture of how grief and worship can cohabitate. We can sit in one and still fall to our knees in the other. We can cry out with both sorrow and praise in the same breath. It is a shallow and dishonest worship that doesn't acknowledge the heartache carried along with the praise. And it is a hopeless grief that doesn't acknowledge the Lord who is worthy of blessing, even within the sadness. Sorrow and worship perfect each other into holy grief.

I can feel like my sadness is somehow sinful. Like someone who truly trusts God would immediately find joy in His plan. But I'm learning that godly grief looks like acknowledging the suffering and the Savior in the same sentence. "Though he slay me, yet will I trust Him" (13:15 NKJV).

Sitting Shiva

Jewish custom provides a beautiful tradition of mourning, called *shiva*, the Hebrew word for "seven." My understanding of it is limited (admittedly, my source is *Grey's Anatomy* and maybe not completely credible), but the gist is seven days of quietly sitting with the mourning family. This mirrors the actions of the three friends of Job who "sat with [Job] on the ground seven days and seven nights, and no one spoke a word to him, for they saw that his suffering was very great" (2:13). Job's friends arrive and do the exactly right thing for seven days: shut up and sit quietly. But things go awry when they start to speak. In the midst of saying a lot of true things about God, they draw a lot of untrue conclusions about Job. They judge him and discourage him and confuse him. In return Job refers to them as "miserable comforters" (16:2). They ultimately are terrible friends to Job, and God makes them sacrifice and repent at the end of the book.[6]

The sad lesson that some of you may need: your people may not know how to help you through your grief. Sometimes your child leaves and your world is rocked, and everyone else just keeps on with normal life. You're a foster parent and you fostered a child and they went home. *That's great. So happy. Job well done.* Or maybe, *So sorry. So sad. Now turn that frown upside down.* Even worse: *You might not be cut out for this. If it's too hard on you, if you can't handle it, maybe you should stop.* Everyone else keeps walking through their days unscathed. Your grief is not understood, not validated. And honestly, you can't expect it to be.

Your grief may be a lonely place, but this stranger wants you to know that I understand, that I'm there with you in it. And so much more than that—more important, more real, more comforting—God is there with you. When you sit with a broken heart, you sit in a beautiful place because—though you may feel alone—it is there that He is closest.[7]

Questioning God

We know that Job was a man who "feared God" (1:1), and the book of Job affords us the privilege of watching a God-fearer wrestle and question his way through trial. Job vacillates back and forth between every human emotion. He questions his own heart: "Shall we receive good from God, and shall we not receive evil?" (2:10). But then he quits trying altogether: "I loathe my life; I would not live forever" (7:16). He swings from challenging God to worshiping God, asking, "Why do you hide your face and count me as your enemy?" (13:24). But then he reassures himself, "I know that my Redeemer lives" (19:25). Job fights with himself and His God to remain faithful and reverent, even in the midst of his questions.

Walking through hard things is not always as simple as arriving at the right conclusion. It often includes wrestling and questioning and cycling through sorrow and confusion. Many of Job's questions and conclusions about God are inaccurate, but at the end of the book, God both rebukes Job's friends and commends Job to them with these words: "You have not spoken the truth about me, *as my servant Job has*" (42:7 NIV, emphasis mine). Certainly not all the words Job spoke about God were true, but God approved of them because they were ultimately spoken with a fear of Him. Our questions can be faith-filled and even worshipful when they're directed *to* God in *faith* rather than *at* God in *accusation*. Even as Job argued with his friends, he couldn't seem to help himself from continually falling back into speaking to God directly—questioning, struggling, worshiping, then questioning and struggling all over again—bringing his pain to the One he knew had the answer.

You will have questions. Heartaches that bring wonder. Turmoil that brings confusion. Direct those questions to your

Father. Bring them to Him directly in fear and faithfulness. God can handle your questions. And when you bring them to Him, you may not find the answers, but you will find Him.

Brace Yourself Like a Man

After thirty-seven chapters of enduring Job and his friends speaking about Him, God enters the scene, and He has something to say: "Who is this that obscures my plans with words without knowledge? Brace yourself like a man; I will question you, and you shall answer me" (38:2–3 NIV).

Then with a hint of sarcasm that I wouldn't exactly expect from God, He asks, "Where were you when I laid the earth's foundation?" (38:4 NIV), and this question pretty much sums up the tone of His soliloquy. "Where were you? Who are you? Can you? Will you?" All these questions point to a fact that Job and his friends seemed to forget: they are not God. God speaks about His power, His sovereignty over all creation, His jurisdiction as the God of justice. He uses images of snow and the mountain goat and everything else in between to display His mighty formation and control of creation. In one fell swoop, God reminds Job of His greatness and Job's smallness. God doesn't necessarily answer Job's questions, but He does respond.

Job is humbled. He eats his words, so to speak. "Surely I spoke of things I did not understand, things too wonderful for me to know . . . therefore, I despise myself and repent" (42:3, 6 NIV). Job didn't receive a direct answer to the many chapters of a long-winded "Why?" But he received exactly what He needed. He *saw* God. "My ears had heard of you but now my eyes have seen you" (42:5 NIV). The same God who spoke to Job through a storm speaks to us through His Word. May we approach Him there with our questions and receive the gift of seeing Him.

In the end, "The LORD blessed the latter part of Job's life more than the former part" (42:12 NIV). But can I just be honest? You might not get the happy ending that Job got. And you almost certainly won't get the voice of the Lord, speaking through a storm and explaining everything. But really, you have exactly what our friend Job had. You have a God who can handle your questions. You have access to the Creator of the universe whom you can approach—with fear and faith—to wrestle with. And you have the very words spoken by God to Job (and every other word of Scripture written before and after) to see God's character as Job did.

Jesus and Grief

Job is a great example of dealing with grief, sure, but who better to look to than Jesus Himself? We get a marvelous picture into godly grief when we read of the death of Jesus's friend Lazarus. Jesus heard the news of His friend's death, and then, as John 11:35 states in the famously short and to-the-point verse, "Jesus wept."

Jesus—God—was faced with sadness, and He responded in the most human way possible: He cried. Of course Jesus knew that Lazarus would be raised to life in a few short minutes— that He would be the One to do it Himself! Jesus knew that this was all part of the plan for Him—for God—to be glorified. Still, His heart was overwhelmed with sadness and His emotions overflowed in tears. Jesus, the sinless One, God Himself, wept in grief over the loss of someone He loved. That tells us that grief is not wrong. In fact, it is very right. Pre-curse, when creation thrived in perfection, there was no loss. Jesus was broken over the reality of death and allowed Himself to be overcome with the human experience of sadness. This two-word verse serves as the blueprint for holy grief. Jesus allowed His emotion and remembered His God. That is what I strive for in my sadness.

Grief is found by accident throughout the day, much like the small symbols that usher it in. A baby sock found behind the dryer. A toothbrush discovered in the medicine cabinet. A Christmas ornament placed on the tree with one name no longer accounted for. It feels like a punch in the gut each time. It swipes the smile off my face without fail. Along with many of you, saying goodbye to children who were once mine has made up the greatest heartaches of my life.

But, oh, my God knows about giving up a child. My God knows about sacrificial love, and it is His sacrificial love that motivates me. He isn't simply the motivation, however. He is also the strength, the sustenance, the comfort. He's the One who called me in, carries me through, and is near always. The One who brought this child into my home—who was with us throughout—is the One who helps me now. God is near to the brokenhearted.[8] God is close to the foster parent.[9]

eighteen

Spectator Signs for the Race

Did you know that you can get an F in gym? You can. I'm living, breathing proof of it. Start with a naturally sedentary person, add in a bit of seventh-grade angst and a touch of asthma, and you've found your winning combo. The key to failing is not to dress for gym at all. Each week when it was time to run the track, I'd decide, "Nah, I'm out," and sit contentedly, dressed in my bell-bottom jeans, on the bleachers.

In eighth grade I met my best friend Julie. Julie went on walks for fun, with no destination, and she expected me to join her. It wasn't happening. So she devised a plan to lure me in. We'd walk to Dunkin' Donuts, where I'd receive the reward of a donut, then past Thornhill Road, where my crush lived. The promise of fried-and-glazed bread and a possible glimpse of Alan Finn (Recognize the name? Yeah, he became my husband) was enough for me. I would go for a walk.

See, Julie knew that for me to be willing to put in the exhausting, sweaty work of exercise, I wasn't going to just go for a walk. I needed a destination.

Run for Your Life

Running is a very biblical metaphor. Paul wrote about running well and not running in vain.[1] At the end of his life, in 2 Timothy 4:7, he said, "I have finished the race." In these verses, Paul is talking at once to you runners who get it and to the people like me who need to be reminded of the destination. "Do you not know that in a race all the runners run, but only one gets the prize? Run in such a way as to get the prize. Everyone who competes in the games goes into strict training. They do it to get a crown that will not last, but we do it to get a crown that will last forever" (1 Corinthians 9:24–25 NIV).

Paul was speaking of a life lived for the glory of Christ. And isn't that what this whole foster parenting thing is about in the first place? We live a life for Him and for others; we run the race and pursue the prize.

While "runner" I am not, "join along in anything fun and celebrate" I am. So, consider me the spectator in the stands, flashing the "Keep Running" signs for you, reminders of the final destination as you run this race.

Sign 1: One Day We Are Going to See God Face-to-Face and Everything Is Going to Make Sense

For now we see only a reflection as in a mirror; then we shall see face to face. Now I know in part; then I shall know fully, even as I am fully known. (1 Corinthians 13:12 NIV)

I've spent the majority of my parenting career confused. There was a time when I felt like I knew what I was doing as a parent. My only daughter was about six months old, and she was in the sweet spot of sleeping through the night but not yet walking. *I've got this thing down*, I thought. But of course, "God opposes the proud" (James 4:6; 1 Peter 5:5) and the like.

Add in walking and temper tantrums, more kids, and then foster care, and I was done for. In case you're wondering, I've spent the past twelve years utterly baffled.

This verse is a part of 1 Corinthians 13, widely known as the Love Chapter. It acknowledges that loving people will put a longing in our hearts to understand the questions attached to the people we're loving.

The questions that plague our hearts are deep and heavy: *What ever happened to that child who left, the one I loved and never saw again? Did I do enough to promote reunification? Why was that child moved from my home, only to bounce around from placement to placement? Is foster parenting having a negative effect on my children, my marriage? Why is there so much brokenness, so much sadness? God, why do You allow this?*

Friends, these questions—and whatever questions you hold in your heart—are questions that, one day, we'll get to ask our heavenly Father face-to-face. One day we won't see through the distorted, fun-house-mirrorlike reflection. We will be with Him, and we will finally, fully know. We'll understand what He was doing, and we'll worship Him for it.

Right now we live in the underbelly of the tapestry that God is weaving. We see the broken threads, clashing colors, distorted picture. It doesn't make sense, and we wouldn't name it "good." But He is the Artist, intentionally and artfully threading each person and plot to create a beautiful piece. One day, in heaven, we will look from above and see the full picture. We will behold the full tapestry in all its glory, we will notice every perfectly placed detail, and we will rejoice.

Sign 2: God Is Making Everything New

He who was seated on the throne said, "Behold, I am making all things new." (Revelation 21:5)

Oh, friend, take heart, *God is making all things new*. Few things elicit the cry of "Come, Lord Jesus!" like rape wounds on a child, like an eight-month-old with a broken leg and X-rays that show old breaks, like holding your child as they scream at night in terror.

We hold the hope that this brokenness and sadness won't last, that one day "He will wipe every tear from their eyes. There will be no more death or mourning or crying or pain" (Revelation 21:4 NIV). Have you cried over your children in the past month? *Today?* One day God Himself will wipe away those tears. This world as we know it is passing away, and every bit of sorrow and brokenness we come in contact with is coming to an end as well.

This hopeful truth is for our children too. If they come to know Christ as their Savior, these truths will salve their hearts as well. We use the term *forever home* to mean the house and family a child ultimately ends up in. It's a beautiful idea, but it's not really an accurate term because nothing about this world is forever. One day we will be "*at home* with the Lord" (2 Corinthians 5:8, emphasis mine). God places within us a longing for the place He created us for. When our kids mourn their first families and crave "home," we can sit with them and mourn with them, but we can also believe for them and with them that, ultimately, this craving is for their *forever* forever home. They will one day feel fully at home in heaven with their Father God. I have a reminder on my mantel to myself, my children, and everyone who reads the words: "If we find ourselves with a desire that nothing in this world can satisfy, the most probable explanation is that we were made for another world."[2]

Foster parents, we know just how broken this world is. We see how sin has destroyed families, how it has decimated the way that things were supposed to be. But we can take heart because this world, as it is, is passing away. It's not going to be this way forever, and we crave the day when it will be made new. Come, Lord Jesus!

Sign 3: The Desires of This World Are Passing Away

This world and its desires pass away, but whoever does the will of God lives forever. (1 John 2:17 NIV)

We get this in our bones, that the desires of this world won't last. We know it for our children with their "I need this [new trendy thing that YouTube told me to love] to be happy" and their middle school love affairs. We can look at them with pity and remember the times we stood in their place (I'm looking at you, Tamagotchi and Matt Fisher). We know how passing those desires are. But we experience them ourselves now as well. The times we buy the perfect shirt and it shrinks to an unwearable size or we eat the perfect meal and are stuffed yet hungry again the next morning. Nothing about this world ultimately fills and satisfies. Every desire—left unfulfilled or temporarily satiated—is passing away.

Oh, what freedom living for God's will instead of the desires of this world brings! When we remember the hope of heaven, we're freed from our slavery to the desires of this world. And the reminder that it's all passing away—even the good things—gives perspective to the things that we're giving up, the costs of foster care.

The thing about survival mode is that you don't know you're in it until you're out of it. Four years ago I was deep in survival mode. I had six kids, ages eight and under. I was homeschooling a third grader and a kindergartner. I had a child with ADHD and impulse-control and behavioral issues, a child who was struggling so severely with sensory processing and emotional dysregulation issues that she cried for five hours a day, and a premature infant who had spent four months in the NICU before joining our family. Four kids were in diapers, one was crawling, and three were in therapy. Add in a wicked custody battle plus the visits and appointments and lawyers and workers and paperwork of two foster children.

I stopped leaving the house. I missed out on playdates and husband dates. Every outing required a double stroller, a single stroller, and a baby wrap and was sure to end with all of us in tears. A whole summer passed without visiting the beach (my favorite place) or Target (my second favorite place). And in case you're wondering, people don't invite "Chaos, party of eight" over for dinner. I had given up much of what had previously made my life full and sweet. Yet this bedrock truth grounded each sacrifice: *All this is passing away, and I want to live for what lasts forever.*

What costs have you experienced as a foster parent? Have you given up things that were precious to you? How about freedom, time, other pursuits, energy and rest, relationships, ease?

We give up a lot for our kids. But the things we give up are earthly things that are passing away. When we have the hope of something greater, those things come into perspective and find their rightful place in our hearts. We experience, along with Jim Elliot, that "he is no fool who gives what he cannot keep to gain what he cannot lose."[3]

Sign 4: Your Work as a Foster and Adoptive Parent Echoes into Eternity

For our light and momentary troubles are achieving for us an eternal glory that far outweighs them all. So we fix our eyes not on what is seen, but on what is unseen, since what is seen is temporary, but what is unseen is eternal. (2 Corinthians 4:17–18 NIV)

Oh, friends, we know "temporary." "Temporary" touches our lives in a profound way.

We give our hearts and souls and sleep and time, and then, in a moment, the little people we gave them to are gone. And we're left with the hours and tears all spent up and gone forever. Sometimes we celebrate, sometimes we mourn, most often we do both. But there are times when it feels like all we've done is meaningless. And if I were left with only what I see—with the temporary of this world and of foster care—the deepest parts of my heart would be tempted to ask, *What is the point of giving up so much for these kids if they're just going to leave?*

But *this* is not all there is. My day-to-day—all that is done and undone, the temporariness, all that joins and then leaves—is not what it seems. There's a whole other realm of "unseen." The unseen—but oh so real—of God's purposes: for entire families' histories to be reoriented and transformed. For the trajectories of children's lives to be radically changed. For souls to be eternally affected. For waves of compassion to flow from our homes and through our communities. God is doing things that we cannot see.

Of course it's easier to see what we can see, right? It's awfully counterintuitive to talk about using the organs created for sight to "see" what can't be seen. But nevertheless, we fight to fix our eyes—the eyes of our minds, our hearts, our beliefs—on what is unseen, because that is what is most real. It's what is eternal.

And Paul reminds us in the passage above that the unseen is the place of "eternal glory." We're so used to reading about God's glory that we assume Paul is inspiring us with a reminder of *God's* glory. But this verse, my friends, is talking to *us* about *our* glory—our troubles are "achieving for *us*" a glory that will overwhelm every one of them. And that leads to my next sign.

Sign 5: God Sees It All

You are the God who sees me. (Genesis 16:13 NIV)

God is not unjust; he will not forget your work and the love you have shown him as you have helped his people and continue to help them. (Hebrews 6:10 NIV)

So much of what we do is unseen. I wish I could hop off these pages and into your real life. I wish I could hide in the corner and "see" you (okay, that's a little creepy) as you work and love. *You spoke patiently to that worker who didn't show up and didn't call. You looked with eyes of love at the child who screamed, "I hate you!" You rocked the baby through the night while the rest of the house slept soundly. You answered with kindness the biological parent who came at you with accusation. You spent hours prepping for an IEP meeting.* I wish I could watch and whisper, "That was a miracle! That was a beautiful expression of love for your Savior! That should be noticed and celebrated and honored! *I saw that!*"

Friend, hear me please: Every moment is noticed. The hard and the mundane—God sees it all. You don't need me to watch and cheer you on. You have the God of the universe watching you. That audience of One sees everything you do and applauds, for it brings Him great joy. And He promises to one day reward you for it.

The menial, outwardly worthless moments of your day have purpose and echo into eternity. In response to the strangers in the grocery store with their "That must be so rewarding" comments, we say, "Oh, you have no idea." Our work is hard, our tasks thankless, our struggles seemingly unseen. But God sees. And like an excited parent holding a good gift for His child behind His back, He says, "Look, I am coming soon! My reward is with me, and I will give to each person according to what they have done" (Revelation 22:12 NIV).

We hate ulterior motives. A good soul does good only for the sake of goodness, right? But this is a "superspiritualism" that is not informed by the words of our God. The concepts that God uses in connection to our service are thrilling: inheritance, crowns, glory, commendation, reward, harvest, treasure, wages, prize.[4] He uses words of bonuses and bounties, of gifts undeserved yet given. And what kind of God would give these deeply motivating promises of reward and then expect us not to be motivated by them? Oh no, He created within us the very nature of motivation, and He placed these promises in His Book so they would take hold of our hearts. He wants us to be motivated by the gifts He will give in reward for our work.

God reminds us of His rewards because He wants us to remember His rewards. In fact, His role as Rewarder is central to who He is. Hebrews 11:6 tells us, "Without faith it is impossible to please him, for whoever would draw near to God must believe that he exists and that he rewards those who seek him." To please God, we must believe these simple realities: He exists (can't get much simpler than that), and He is a rewarder. His rewarding is such a part of who He is that He says it's impossible to please Him if we don't believe it. So know it and believe it. Your love for your children, your service to their biological families, your work on behalf of the vulnerable are building up rewards for you. Lasting, joyous rewards that you can't even imagine. You are storing for yourself treasures in heaven.[5]

Sign 6: Heaven Is Real

My Father's house has many rooms; if that were not so, would I have told you that I am going there to prepare a place for you? (John 14:2 NIV)

Heaven is a *real* place with *real* people and has a *real* city with *real* dimensions. There, we'll be with the *real* person of Jesus Christ and our *real* heavenly Father who sits on His throne.

If I'm honest, heaven doesn't always feel very real to me. The passing and temporary of this world are what feel real. The rest is more like a child's story, like a kind of make-believe. While it's not make-believe, it does take a level of imagination. As Randy Alcorn writes in his book *In Light of Eternity*, "I believe God expects us to recognize the limits and flaws of our imaginations, but to utilize them nonetheless (remembering always that though we're using our 'imaginations' heaven is more real than anything we've ever seen or touched). If God didn't want us to imagine what heaven will be like, he wouldn't have told us what he has."[6]

A day is coming, the joy and glory and beauty of which we cannot even imagine. But it doesn't mean we can't try.[7] It doesn't mean that we don't lie in our beds and dream of the glories of the place where all will be perfect, that we don't stare off absentmindedly in traffic and imagine the splendor of what it will be like to live with Jesus. We can use our creativity and our vision and our sense of hope to look in anticipation to that day. We can become so heavenly minded that we are *so* earthly good.

This skin I wear confuses my sense of reality. But a day is coming when reality will come into perspective. When we will see face-to-face. When this world and its desires will pass away. When God will wipe away every tear. When we will see the unseen and approach our glory. When we will receive the rewards that He has been storing for us.

One day "the Lord himself will descend from heaven with a cry of command, with the voice of an archangel, and with the sound of the trumpet of God. And the dead in Christ will rise first. Then we who are alive, who are left, will be caught up together with them in the clouds to meet the Lord in the air, and so we will always be with the Lord" (1 Thessalonians 4:16–17). And as we meet the Lord, we will finally see the reality of our eternal forever.

Now Is Your Time for Grief

Jesus doesn't bait and switch His followers—*us*. He is clear that trouble will come. Right before He died, He warned His disciples of the trouble they were about to face, namely, "You will see me no longer" (John 16:16). Of course, this is the place we, as twenty-first-century Christians, live. We don't physically walk with Jesus; we aren't able to see Him. Right now we live in the things hoped for, the conviction of what we cannot see.[8]

> Are you asking one another what I meant when I said, "In a little while you will see me no more, and then after a little while you will see me"? Very truly I tell you, you will weep and mourn while the world rejoices. You will grieve, but *your grief will turn to joy*. A woman giving birth to a child has pain because her time has come; but when her baby is born she forgets the anguish because of her joy that a child is born into the world. So with you: Now is your time of grief, but I will see you again and *you will rejoice, and no one will take away your joy*." (John 16:19–22 NIV, emphasis mine)

I don't have to tell you. In this life, you will weep and mourn. In this foster care life, especially, you will weep and mourn. You will grieve, but, friend, *your grief will turn into joy*. One day we will be with Jesus and see Him, and we will rejoice. After this life of coming and going, of hellos and goodbyes, it will finally be final, completely complete. And no one will be able to take away our joy.

Epilogue

What I Know

In eleven days I find out if my daughter of eighteen months will be leaving me. She won't be leaving to be with her mother, whom I love, or her father, whom I want her to know. A stranger, someone who has staked a claim on her based on a technicality, will take her from the only home and the only family that she has ever known. Last night I whispered in her ear, as I do to each of my children, "I love you more than life." And I couldn't help but wonder how in the world this life of ours will just keep on, but without her. It's unimaginable, unthinkable, unavoidable.

These are the times when I need to *know that I know that I know* that foster parenting is worth it.

Left to myself, I am entirely dominated by fear and pain, a sense of injustice, and a crippling rage. There is no time that I need to be brought back to the why of this life more than when I'm bending under the burden of my sorrow. No time I need to be reminded of *all* the second-grade "*Wh*—" questions. I need to remember the what, the why, the who, and the how.

Being consumed by the sadness, fear, and anger is like a reflex. Everything within me goes to those things instinctively, and the inertia of them can bring me to hopelessness and despair. It takes a revolution, a revelation, to fight and to decide. I turn the spout of all that's pouring into my heart and my mind and redirect it. I have to re-believe, to look away from my feelings, my thoughts, my fears, and my concerns. Standing at attention, feet planted, chin up, heart expectant, I turn away from my thoughts and feelings to what I believe, what I know: I know that God created the family. That it's sacred to Him. And that—when at all possible—His heart is for it to be healed and restored. That His plan is for family to live together in love and unity.

I know that because of God I do not have to fear. That His character and His promises and His faithfulness can grant peace when I'm afraid.

I know that God hears my prayers. That He uses my cries to Him to change my heart, that they actually affect the trajectory of my children's lives and the world as I know it.

I know that God is in charge and makes better plans than I ever could. That I never actually hold control, that I can surrender to Him. That He's not only in the storm, but He's above the storm.

I know that God is glorified when I have loved well—when I have loved with a sacrificial love that mirrors His love. That giving my whole heart is never the wrong thing, and that guarding my thoughts will always serve me.

I know that God loves these children's biological parents. That He adores their souls, that they are deeply precious to Him. That before being one who shows grace, I'm one who has received grace.

I know that God has great plans for me—to meet me and transform me—in every step of this foster parenting journey.

That in all the in-betweens and unknowns, He is there with lessons, with work to be done, with His goodness.

I know that every moment I've held, rocked, kissed, fed, spoken to, played with, and nurtured the children in my home has contributed to their physical, emotional, and spiritual healing. That God has used my efforts for the good of these children.

I know that but for the grace of God go I, and that I am no better than my children's parents. That I am the beneficiary of great gifts, the receiver of mercy, the recipient of grace.

I know that God loves my family, my forever children, more than I ever could and has great plans for them, for their good. That He will help and comfort them, just as He helps and comforts me.

I know that God is with my precious foster children when I'm not, when I can't be. That He never leaves them, that He can protect and comfort and rescue. That when they are removed from the safety of my loving watch, they are always under His.

I know that God will bring me to a place of rest. That He will strengthen me as I practice humility, and that He will teach me what it means to live in peace and joy.

I know that the system and the process and the people are all under God's sovereign and good plan. That no person could thwart His will.

I know that God has provided others to walk this journey with me, that there is comfort and strength found in their community. That He has called me to provide comfort and strength to them just the same.

I know that a small-time county judge is really just a human conduit of the great Judge who is always actually deciding the fates of these children. That God is just, and justice is ultimately His.

I know that God is close to the brokenhearted. That He uses my own sorrows to draw me closer to Himself, and that He is with me in my grief.

I know that one day, I will see God and everything will make sense. That I will finally understand, and I will live in the joy of His presence and rewards forever.

When my life feels hard and hopeless, when confusion and grief overwhelm, when my heart is broken and my hands are weary, when I want to give up and I wonder *Why?*—I know then and remind myself always that all this is worth it. I may not feel it, but I believe it, I know it.

I *know* foster care is worth it.

Appendix

Resources for the Trauma-Informed Parent

My favorite must-read for an intro to trauma-informed parenting: *The Connected Child: Bring Hope and Healing to Your Adoptive Family* by Karyn B. Purvis, PhD, David R. Cross, PhD, and Wendy Lyons Sunshine

My favorite practical book for day-to-day trauma-informed parenting: *The Connected Parent: Real-Life Strategies for Building Trust and Attachment* by Karyn Purvis, PhD, and Lisa Qualls

My favorite deep-dive book on the effects of trauma on the body and brain: *The Body Keeps the Score: Brain, Mind, and Body in the Healing of Trauma* by Bessel van der Kolk, MD

My favorite book for understanding our children's sensory needs: *The Out-of-Sync Child: Recognizing and Coping with Sensory Processing Disorder* by Carol Stock Kranowitz, MA

My favorite book for helping our kids with sensory needs: *The Connected Therapist: Relating Through the Senses* by Marti Smith, OTR/L

My favorite foundational book on attachment: *How We Love Our Kids: The Five Love Styles of Parenting* by Milan and Kay Yerkovich

My favorite trauma-informed book on attachment: *Securely Attached: How Understanding Childhood Trauma Will Transform Your Parenting* by Mike and Kristin Berry

My favorite foster care/adoption "handbook": *Wounded Children, Healing Homes: How Traumatized Children Impact Adoptive and Foster Families* by Jayne E. Schooler, Betsy Keefer Smalley, LSW, and Timothy J. Callahan, PsyD

My favorite book about in-utero exposure to drugs and alcohol: *The Mystery of Risk: Drugs, Alcohol, Pregnancy, and the Vulnerable Child* by Ira J. Chasnoff, MD

My favorite book about helping infants who suffer from Neonatal Abstinence Syndrome: *The Happiest Baby on the Block: The New Way to Calm Crying and Help Your Newborn Baby Sleep Longer*, second edition, by Harvey Karp, MD

Notes

Welcome to My Life

1. DCPP stands for Division of Child Protection and Permanency, which is an agency within the New Jersey Department of Children and Families, or DCF. Throughout the book, I use the abbreviations DCPP and DCF somewhat interchangeably.

2. Jamie C. Finn (fosterthefamilyblog), Instagram, November 20, 2019, https://www.instagram.com/p/B5G8E3hliK9/.

Chapter 2 Jesus Loves the Little Children (and Their Families)

1. I recognize that some of the terms throughout this book are problematic. For example, I use the terms *foster children* and *my/your children* interchangeably for brevity and clarity's sake, recognizing that neither label is ideal. The best term would probably be *child in foster care*, but it would be very difficult to use such a clunky phrase throughout the book. The same applies to terms relating to biological parents, caseworkers, and the like. Please hear that these terms are written with respect and care, and I simplify them only in an attempt to be as succinct as possible.

Chapter 3 Do Not Be Afraid (When Everything Is Scary)

1. See Deuteronomy 31:8.

2. See Romans 8:28.

3. Amy DiMarcangelo, *A Hunger for More: Finding Satisfaction in Jesus When the Good Life Doesn't Fill You* (Wheaton: Crossway, forthcoming), chap. 8.

Chapter 4 I Don't Even Know How to Pray Anymore

1. See John 4:7–15.
2. See Matthew 8:23–27.
3. See Luke 9:44–46; 18:34.
4. See, for example, Mark 2:1–12.
5. See Matthew 7:7; John 15:7; 1 John 5:14–15.
6. Prayer inspired by Joshua 1:5, 9.
7. Prayer inspired by Matthew 11:28–30 NIV.
8. See Psalm 57:2.
9. See, for example, Luke 11:9; 22:42.
10. See also Matthew 7:7–11; Mark 10:14–16; Luke 10:21.
11. This idea was inspired by Paul Miller, *A Praying Life: Connecting with God in a Distracting World* (Colorado Springs: NavPress, 2017).
12. Miller, *A Praying Life*, 31.
13. See Psalm 139:2, 4.
14. See, for example, James 5:13–15.

Chapter 5 Out of Control

1. See Romans 5:8; Psalms 139:16; 91:11.
2. See 1 Peter 2:13–14.
3. See Romans 13:1.
4. See Proverbs 16:9.
5. See Hebrews 4:16.
6. See Genesis 1:2; Colossians 1:16–17.

Chapter 6 Too Attached

1. Karyn B. Purvis, David R. Cross, and Wendy Lyons Sunshine, *The Connected Child: Bring Hope and Healing to Your Adoptive Family* (New York: McGraw-Hill, 2007).
2. Jayne E. Schooler, Betsy Keefer Smalley, and Timothy J. Callahan, *Wounded Children, Healing Homes: How Traumatized Children Impact Adoptive and Foster Families* (Colorado Springs: NavPress, 2009), 62–65.
3. This idea was articulated by my friend Rachel Randolph.
4. Purvis, Cross, and Sunshine, *Connected Child*.
5. Of course, children in foster care have experienced trauma, abuse, or neglect, all of which affect their relational, physiological, and sensory needs. The key is to meet each child where they are and provide loving care in whatever ways will most help them and communicate love to them.
6. See Romans 2:1.
7. See Ephesians 4:22.
8. See Philippians 4:13.
9. See 1 Corinthians 4:7.

10. See Psalm 139:16 NIV.
11. D. Martyn Lloyd-Jones, *Spiritual Depression: Its Causes and Cure* (Grand Rapids: Eerdmans, 1965), 20.
12. See Lamentations 3:42.
13. See Romans 8:28.

Chapter 7 My Foster Child's Family Is My Enemy

1. See James 3:1–12.
2. See Ephesians 2:1; Philippians 4:13.

Chapter 8 God Is in the Wait

1. David Platt, *Radical: Taking Back Your Faith from the American Dream* (Colorado Springs: Multnomah, 2010).
2. See Genesis 12:1–20.
3. See Genesis 12:12–13; 20:2.
4. See Genesis 16.
5. See Genesis 17:17; 18:12.
6. See Genesis 18:14.
7. See Psalm 139:16.
8. See Romans 8:29; 2 Corinthians 3:18.
9. See John 15:2.
10. See Philippians 1:6.
11. See 2 Peter 3:8.
12. See Psalm 65:8; 2 Corinthians 6:2; Ecclesiastes 3.
13. See Psalm 31:15.

Chapter 9 I Thought My Love Would Be Enough

1. Check the appendix for a list of resources for parenting children who have experienced trauma and in-utero exposure.
2. See John 16:7–15.
3. See 1 John 3:1.
4. See Colossians 3:14.
5. See Romans 8:35–39.
6. See Psalm 139:7–12.
7. See 1 Timothy 1:15.
8. See Philippians 1:6.
9. Ann Voskamp, "The Broken Way" (presentation, Refresh Conference, Overlake Christian Church, Seattle, WA, March 2, 2018).

Chapter 10 What Do You Have That You Did Not Receive?

1. See Luke 12:48.
2. See Micah 6:8 NIV.

3. See Luke 6:36.
4. See 1 Corinthians 16:14.

Chapter 11 But What about My Kids?

1. See Ephesians 2:10.
2. See Deuteronomy 11:19; Proverbs 22:6.
3. Corrie ten Boom, *The Hiding Place* (Grand Rapids: Chosen Books, 2006), 42.
4. See 1 Timothy 3:4–5; 5:8.

Chapter 12 I Don't Want to Hand Her Over Today

1. See Psalm 139:5.
2. See Psalm 139:7–8.
3. See Psalm 100:3.
4. See Philippians 4:13.

Chapter 13 Self-Care Isn't Selfish

1. "Secondary Traumatic Stress," Administration for Children and Families, accessed May 20, 2020, www.acf.hhs.gov/trauma-toolkit/secondary-traumatic-stress.
2. If you think you may be experiencing secondary trauma, please consider getting professional help from a medical doctor and/or a counselor.
3. See Titus 2:4 NIV.
4. See 1 Peter 4:10.
5. See Mark 4:35–38.
6. See Matthew 4:18; 5:1; 12:1; Mark 2:13; Luke 6:1.
7. See Psalm 100:4; 1 Timothy 4:4.
8. See Job 2:10.
9. See Romans 8:28.
10. Saint Augustine, *Confessions*, 1.1.1.

Chapter 14 Social Workers and Therapists and Lawyers—Oh My!

1. See Ephesians 2:10.
2. See 1 John 3:15.
3. See Colossians 2:14.
4. See 1 Peter 5:7.

Chapter 15 Foster-Caring Community

1. See John 13:34.
2. See Colossians 3:16; Ephesians 4:11–13; Hebrews 10:24–25.
3. See 1 Peter 5:5.

4. Jeffrey Kranz, "All the 'One Another' Commands in the NT," Overview Bible, March 9, 2014, http://overviewbible.com/one-another-infographic/.

5. See Proverbs 27:6.

6. See 1 Peter 5:5.

Chapter 16 A Small-Time County Judge

1. See Psalm 7:11; Romans 14:10.

2. See Acts 17:31; Isaiah 61:8.

3. "28 U.S. Code § 453 Oaths of Justices and Judges," Legal Information Institute, Cornell Law School, accessed May 20, 2020, www.law.cornell.edu /uscode/text/28/453.

4. See Acts 5:29, 40–42; Exodus 1:17–21; Joshua 2:1–7; Daniel 3:16–29 for examples of God-honoring civil disobedience and radical action in the face of injustice.

Chapter 17 Foster Care Is Heartbreak

1. I hope by now you understand my heart for family preservation and reunification. While we celebrate a family being made whole, these feelings of death, a missing child, losing a child who feels like "yours" are common feelings foster parents experience.

2. Alfred, Lord Tennyson, "In Memoriam A.H.H. OBIIT MDCCCXXXIII: 27," Poetry Foundation, https://www.poetryfoundation.org/poems/45336/in -memoriam-a-h-h-obiit-mdcccxxxiii-27.

3. See Psalm 56:8.

4. See 2 Corinthians 4:17; Romans 8:18.

5. Michael Rosen, *We're Going on a Bear Hunt* (New York: Aladdin Paperbacks, 2003).

6. See Job 42:8.

7. See Psalm 34:18.

8. See Psalm 34:18.

9. You may need professional help working through your grief, especially if you don't have others in your life who can understand and walk through it with you. I know many foster parents who are in therapy—I am myself! If you feel weighed down by your grief, please consider finding professional help.

Chapter 18 Spectator Signs for the Race

1. See Galatians 5:7; Philippians 2:16.

2. C. S. Lewis, *Mere Christianity* (New York: HarperOne, 2015), 121.

3. Jim Elliot, *The Journals of Jim Elliot* (Grand Rapids: Revell, 2002), 174.

4. See Colossians 3:23–24; James 1:12; 2 Corinthians 4:17; Matthew 25:21; Matthew 16:27; Galatians 6:9; Luke 12:33; 1 Corinthians 3:8; Philippians 3:14.

5. See Matthew 6:20.

6. Randy Alcorn, *In Light of Eternity: Perspectives on Heaven* (Colorado Springs: WaterBrook, 1999), 24.

7. I highly recommend reading nearly any book by Randy Alcorn to build your enthusiasm for heaven. He writes fiction and nonfiction books that inspire the reader to joyfully imagine and anticipate heaven.

8. See Hebrews 11:1.

Jamie C. Finn is the executive director of Foster the Family, the host of the *Real Mom* podcast, the founder and owner of Goods and Better, and a sought-after speaker for retreats, conferences, and events for foster and adoptive parents. Her popular social media accounts offer a glimpse into the real life of a foster parent and provide encouragement to thousands of foster parents. At any given moment, Jamie is a mother to four to six children, including her two biological children and two children adopted through foster care. She lives in Sicklerville, New Jersey, with them and her husband, Alan.

For More Encouragement and Support, Connect with Jamie

 @fosterthefamilyblog

Learn more at **fosterthefamilyblog.com**

Gear and Goods That Benefit Foster Children

GOODS & BETTER
GOODS AND GEAR ON A MISSION

BUY IT FORWARD

1

BUY YOUR GOODS
Grab something you love.

2

CHOOSE YOUR IMPACT
Proceeds from your purchase benefit a child entering foster care. Choose how at checkout.

3

LEAVE THE BETTER TO US
We donate & deliver something special to a foster child on your behalf.

Start shopping

→

YOU CHOOSE YOUR IMPACT.
every purchase benefits a child in foster care

Printed in the United States
by Baker & Taylor Publisher Services